CLEP

Western Civilization I
2012

Condensed Summary and Test Prep Guide

By David C. Haus and Michael D. Haus

Copyright ©2012
All Rights Reserved
Printed in the USA

ISBN:# 978-1611045949

Published by:

Feather Trail Press, LLC
P. O. Box 7
Cedar Lake, Michigan 48812

Table of Contents

Nations and other Geographic Places 5

Cities 13

Buildings and Landmarks 18

Cultural Artifacts 24

Political Powers and Dynasties 25

Legislative Bodies 29

Legal Codes 32

Systems of Government 34

Political Offices and Titles 38

People 39

Painters, Poets and Writers (Renaissance) 87

Explorers and Scientists 91

Cultures 94

Languages 102

Social and Cultural Facts 104

Innovations, Technology, and Achievements 108

Diseases and Plagues 112

Business Facts 113

People Groups (Entertainers) 116

People Groups (Political) 118

People Groups (Religious) 120
People Groups (Social Classes) 122

Painting and Sculpture 123
Literary Facts and Forms 124
Literary Works 126

Religions 129
Gods 130
Mythological Beliefs 132
Philosophical and Religious Concepts and Beliefs 134
Social and Religious Movements 137
Religious and Philosophic Texts 138

Battles and Wars 140
Other Disputes 146
Military Facts 148
Treaties and Leagues 150

Quotes and Anecdotes 153
Famous Nicknames 157

Historical Periods and Eras 161
Important Dates in Chronological Order 163

Nations and other Geographic Places

America:

- was first reached by the Vikings (also known as Norsemen or Northmen) as early as the start of the 11th century
- the "Vineland" discovered by the Vikings may have been the New England coast
    - Vineland referred to the grapes discovered there
- the Vikings were likely the first American settlers, though no certain remains of such settlements now exist
- named after Italian explorer Amerigo Vespucci

Antigonid:

- region ruled by a dynasty of Hellenistic kings descended from Alexander the Great's general Antigonus I Monophthalmus
- began after the death of Alexander the Great when his empire was divided into three kingdoms

Assyria:

- remained a minor Akkadian province for many years
- conquered Babylonia around 1300 B.C.
- rose to dominance under the rule of Tiglathi-nin
- fully established as an empire around 700 B.C.
- dominated Western Asia from 700 B.C. until the fall of Ninevah in 606 B.C.

CLEP Western Civilization I

Australia:

- was officially discovered in 1770 A.D. by Captain James Cook
    - Europeans suspected a continent in the southern hemisphere for centuries but didn't know how to reach it
    - Portuguese sailors may have sailed along Australia's coast as early as 1542 A.D.

Chaldea, Assyria, and Babylonia:

- rose to prominence as empires in succession
- existed in the Tigris-Euphrates river basin
- vastly expanded their dominions

Corsica:

- French island located west of Italy
- mountainous island formed by volcanic explosions
- fourth largest island in the Mediterranean Sea
- was made a province of Rome until the 5th century when it was conquered by invading tribes

Etruria:

- region of central Italy, in the same area which is now Tuscany
- home to a wealthy and cultured seagoing people who were leaders on their peninsula before the rise of the Romans
- where the art of haruspices or soothsaying was introduced (discovering the divine mind by observing the entrails of sacrificial animals)

Flanders:

- portion of Belgium (the exact location of which has varied throughout the centuries)

Nations and other Geographic Places

Great Britain:

- often escaped invasion due to its island status
- began building a strong navy during the 5th century reign of Henry VII
- eluded the Spanish invasion of 1588 A.D. through the strength of its navy (weather was also a factor)
    - Spain's army was waiting in the Netherlands for a huge armada of ships to come up from the south and transport it over to Britain
    - the British navy prevented the Spanish ships from landing
    - the British ships were lighter and more maneuverable
    - The armada tried to escape by sailing north around Scotland and down the west side of the British Isles but were battered by strong storms
    - only 77 of 141 Spanish ships made it home

Greece:

- became the Macedonian Empire after the conquests of Alexander the Great
- was split after Alexander's death because his generals couldn't agree on a single successor
- was divided into three kingdoms:
    - Ptolemaic
    - Seleucid
    - Antigonid Dynasty

Iceland:

- Nordic European island country in the North Atlantic
- rose to prominence as a literary center of the Scandinavian world
- relied on a class of scalds, or bards who orally transmitted the sagas of the Norse races before the invention of writing
- produced collections of 12th century poems or sagas called Eddas
    - the *Elder Edda* (poetic) and the *Younger Edda* (prose)
        - the *Eddas* are among the most interesting and important literary memorials handed down from the early Teutonic (Germanic tribe) peoples

Israel:

- began as a loose collection of tribes united by their religious beliefs and faith in Yahweh
- experienced the following major historic events:
    - sojourn of Jacob's descendants in Egypt
    - exodus of the Hebrews from Egypt
    - issuance of The Ten Commandments from Mt. Sinai
    - conquest of Canaan
    - apportionment of the conquered land among the 12 tribes of Israel

Macedonia:

- ancient kingdom located in the northeastern part of the Greek peninsula
- first became prominent under the military leadership of Philip II of Macedon (father of Alexander the Great)
- fragmented after the death of Alexander the Great

Nations and other Geographic Places

Mesopotamia:

- land between the Euphrates and Tigris rivers (Tigris-Euphrates river basin)
- the cradle of civilization
- home to the Sumerians, Akkadians, Babylonians, Assyrians, Chaldeans, and to some degree the Hittites, Phoenicians and Persians

Mount Olympus:

- the most famous mountain of the Greek peninsula
- located in Northern Thessaly
- the highest mountain in Greece, thought by the ancient Greeks to be the world's highest mountain (it is 9700 feet high)
- thought to be the abode of the gods, ruled by a 12-member celestial council of six males and six females which was led by Zeus

Netherland (Dutch Republic):

- bears "United Provinces of the Netherlands" as its official name
- won its independence from Spain in 1609 A.D.
- rose as a world power shortly thereafter
    - merchant shipping and a period of cultural, economic, and scientific growth contributed to the Dutch rise
- sided against the Catholics during the Protestant Reformation

Phoenicia:

- thrived on the coast of the Mediterranean Sea, near Mount Lebanon
- famous for:
    - fine fir timber cut from the forests of Lebanon
    - the "cedars of Lebanon," which held a prominent place in the history and poetry of the East
    - Tyrian purple (a purple-red dye named after the city of Tyre)
- provided King Solomon with craftsmen and timber for his magnificent temple
- delivered timber for the construction of the great palaces and temples of the Assyrians, Babylonians, and Egyptians
- provided ships to the Persian kings for wars against Asia Minor and Europe

Portugal:

- borders the Atlantic and Spain
- won independence from Spain in 1639 A.D.
- led by its navigators (Henry the Navigator, Vasco da Gama etc...), expanded western influence and established a global empire during the Age of Discovery

Ptolemaic Kingdom:

- began after the death of Alexander the Great when his empire was divided into three kingdoms
- flourished under a line of kings known as the Ptolomies:
    - each took the name Ptolemy
    - they ruled the Egyptians for the three centuries after Pharaoh Necho II's reign
    - they were willingly accepted by the Egyptians
- ended in 30 B.C. when the region was annexed by the Romans

Nations and other Geographic Places

Rome:

- conspired to destroy Carthage (near modern day Tunis) after destroying Macedonia and Corinth, even though the city was under Rome's protection
- repeatedly betrayed the city of Carthage, finally burning it under the leadership of Scipio Aemilianus (who later destroyed the Numanitan city of Spain)
- took 50,000 prisoners in Carthage (the rest of the 700,000 residents had either escaped or been killed)

Russia (Rus):

- was first entered by the Vikings in 862 A.D., in response to the request of the Slavs in Novgorod who asked them to bring order to their settlement
    - the Vikings were led by Rurik, who was treated in a kingly fashion and founded the first royal line in Russia
- boasts Kievan Rus (medieval Slavic state – forerunner of modern Russia) which grew up around the town of Kiev and was ruled by Oleg
- was profoundly impacted by Byzantine culture in the areas of art, architecture, literature, and epic poetry
- felt the great influence of Orthodox Christianity, although religion played a different role in Russia than it did in Western history

Seleucid:

- comprised almost all the countries of Asia conquered by Alexander, stretching from the Hellespont to the Indus
- was ruled by Seleucus Nicator:
    - a ruler of unusual ability
    - liberal patron of learning and art
    - reputedly "the greatest founder of cities that ever lived"

Spain:

- fell to the Visigoths sometime after 700 A.D.
    - the royal family converted to Catholicism at about that time
- emerged as a unified country in the 15th century.
- dominated Europe as a leading power throughout the 16th and most of the 17th century

Switzerland:

- is situated in a landlocked area of western Europe
- began its march towards independence when the Swiss Army defeated the Austrians in three different battles:
    - Battle of Morgarten Pass (1315 A.D.)
    - Battle of Sempach (1386 A.D.)
    - Battle of Näfels (1388 A.D.)

Cities

Alexandria (Egypt):

- city founded by Alexander the Great and named for himself
- located in the northern part of the country along the Mediterranean sea
- known for the Lighthouse of Alexandria, one of the Seven Wonders of the World and it's library which was the largest in the ancient world

Amsterdam (Netherlands):

- the Netherlands are located on Germany's northwestern border. The city of Amsterdam
  is located in the west central part of the country.
- the center of trade in the emerging world economy of the 16th century
    - The Amsterdam Exchange (now renamed the Amsterdam Stock Exchange)
        - opened in 1609 A.D.
        - became the focus of intra-European and intercontinental trade
        - is considered to be the oldest stock exchange in the world

Antwerp (Belgium):

- Belgium - small nation located on France's northern border. The city of Antwerp is located in north central Belgium
- became the main banking and financial city in Northern Europe in the 16th century
- received Portuguese merchant ships carrying spices from the East Indies in 1501 A.D.
    - these ships avoided the Italian ports altogether, resulting in the rise of Antwerp as an important shipping port
- was hit hard economically in 1557 A.D. by the partial bankruptcy of Spain, leading to the rise in prominence of Genoa, Italy

Athens (Greece)

- located in southeastern Greece
- capital and largest city of Greece
- widely referred to as the cradle of Western civilization
- the birthplace of democracy

Baghdad (Iraq):

- located on the lower Tigris River
- established as the royal residence of the Abbasside dynasty of Caliphs
- remained the home of the Abbasside Caliphs for a period of five hundred years—until the subversion of the house by the Tartars of the North
- enjoyed a Golden Age, during which time the culture, philosophy, and luxury of the Arabs outshined the rogue empires of Christendom
    - this Golden Age was illustrated by the reign of Haroun-al-Raschid, hero of Arabian Nights

Bruges (Belgium):

- a city in Flanders (present day Belgium) – located in northwestern side of country near the coast.
- one of the most important trading cities in Europe from 1200-1500 A.D.
- reached a population of almost 100,000 by 1450 A.D.
- famous for the production of a much coveted, high quality woolen cloth which manufactured from English wool and traded all over Europe

Cologne (Germany):

- located in west central part of the country (currently the fourth largest city in Germany)
- founded as a Roman settlement
- grew quickly after 900 A.D., becoming the largest city in Germany by the 12th century
- home to the University of Cologne, one of the oldest universities in Europe (founded in 1388 A.D.)

Constantinople (Turkey):

- originally called Byzantium
- located on the Bosporous River (modern day Istanbul)
- selected as the new capital of the Roman empire by Constantine (it was named after him and also known as the "City of Constantine"
    - reasons for the change in capital city:
        - the ungracious conduct of the citizens of Rome, who were unhappy because Constantine had abandoned the worship of the old deities
        - a shift eastward in the Roman empire's population center, wealth, and culture (due to conquests in that direction)
- eluded being conquered by the Arabs for several centuries longer than Alexandria
- thwarted the first Arab attack in 668 A.D. through the use of a bituminous compound called Greek Fire
- thwarted a siege by a powerful Muslim army in 716 A.D. with a heroic defense by Emperor Leo III
- lasted as a Latin empire for only 50 years after the Fourth Crusade
- changed hands in 1261 A.D. when the Greeks regained the throne
- was ruled by the Greeks until captured by the Turks in 1453 A.D.

Florence (Italy):

- located in central Italy
- served as a great manufacturing, financial, art, and literary center of the Middle Ages
- included many illustrious citizens, including Machiavelli, Michael Angelo, Leonardo da Vinci, Galileo, Amerigo Vespucci, and the Medici family

Genoa (Italy):

- an important European financial center
- a major seaport on the northwestern coast of Italy

Tyre (Lebanon):

- located on the eastern side of the Mediterranean sea
- the only Phoenician city that closed its gates against the advances of Alexander the Great
- fell to Alexander after a siege in 332 B.C.
- now "bare as the top of a rock" (as predicted in the Old Testament book of Ezekiel), a place where fishermen spread their nets to dry

Venice (Italy):

- located on the northeastern coast of Italy
- started as a camp for penniless refugees who fled to the marshes of the Adriatic to escape Attila the Hun
- celebrated her supremacy on the sea annually by dropping a ring into the sea in brilliant ceremony called "Wedding the Adriatic"
- lost much of its territory east of the Adriatic due to 15th century Turkish invasions
- a great center of commerce until the voyage of Vasco da Gama around the Cape of Good Hope (1497-8 A.D.) which showed a new path to India which did not go through Venice

Buildings and Landmarks

Cathedrals:

- were tall, graceful, and built in the Romanesque style during medieval times
- developed into the Gothic style, which was built between the 12th and 16th centuries A.D., and included the:
    - cathedral in Burgos in Spain, which was built in 1221 A.D. (though it's ornate Gothic towers were added later
    - castle of Notre Dame in Paris (begun in 1163 A.D.)

Cheops (The Great Pyramid of Giza):

- the oldest and largest Egyptian pyramid
- thought to be the largest building ever constructed
- started by the pharaoh Cheops (Khufu I) around 2700 B.C.
- one of the "Seven Wonders of the Ancient World"
- located near Cairo

Medieval castles:

- were generally surrounded by a body of water called a moat
- featured a drawbridge that could be raised when the castle was under attack to keep the enemy from crossing the moat

Monasteries:

- were built as a place to avoid temptation and sin
- began to spread and flourish in the 4th century A.D.
- existed before that time, but not in such popularity or numbers

Seven Wonders of the Ancient World:

- refers to remarkable constructions of classical antiquity listed by various authors in guidebooks popular among the ancient Hellenic tourists, including:
    - Great Pyramid of Giza
    - Hanging Gardens of Babylon
    - Temple of Artemis at Ephesus
    - Statute of Zeus at Olympia
    - Mausoleum of Halicarnassus
    - Colossus of Rhodes
    - Lighthouse of Alexandria

The Arch of Constantine:

- commemorated the victory of Constantine over his rival, Maxentius (an event which established Christianity as the imperial and favored religion of the Roman empire)
- was constructed with single and triple archways
- was modeled after the city gates

The Catacombs were:

- where many Christians hid, lived, and buried their dead, and sketched crude symbols of their hope and faith during the terrible persecution by the emperor Diocletian (303-311 A.D.)
- comprised of vast subterranean galleries and chambers under the city of Rome
- where Christian art had its beginnings

The Colosseum (also known as the Flavian Amphitheatre) was:

- begun by the Roman emperor Vespasian
- completed and dedicated by Titus, who was Vespasian's son and successor
- capable of accommodating more than 80,000 spectators
- used for various purpose, including housing, workshops, quarters for a religious order, and as a Christian shrine

The Colossus of Rhodes:

- was sculpted by Chares (a great Greek sculptor and the most noted pupil of Lysippus, another Greek sculptor)
- was an enormous bronze statue of the sun god Helios
- sculpted in 280 B.C.
- was about 107 feet high
- stood for more than 50 years before collapsing during an earthquake
- lay prone on the ground for more than 900 years
- Rhodes is an island of the Southwestern coast of Asia Minor

The Egyptian temple of Ipsambul:

- is a remarkable, rock-hewn structure
- features four huge (70-foot) portrait-statues of Ramses II across the facade
- has been called one of the grandest achievements of Egyptian art
- is located in Nubia (beyond the First Cataract of the Nile).

The Great Rock of Behistun:

- records the achievements of Darius the Great in three parallel columns
- is inscribed in cuneiform characters and in three languages
    - Aryan
    - Turanian
    - Semitic
- is the equivalent of the Rosetta Stone for enabling translation of those three languages

The Hanging Gardens of Nebuchadnezzar II:

- were built for his Median wife, Amytis, who missed the mountain scenery of her homeland
- simulated the appearance of a mountain rising in cultivated terraces towards the eastern sky
- were greatly admired by the ancient Greeks

Buildings and Landmarks

The Long Walls:

- were great ramparts, 4-5 miles long, which linked Athens to the ports of Piraeus and Phalerum
- were built in Athens at the urging of Pericles
- effectively converted Athens and her ports into a vast fortification

The Mausoleum at Halicarnassus:

- was one of the Seven Wonders of The World
- was a monumental tomb erected as a tribute to Mausolus (king of Caria who died in 353 B.C.), his wife, and sister
- Caria was located in south Asia Minor (modern day Turkey)
- was erected by Mausolus' wife Artemisia, who outlived him by only two years
- was such a grand tomb that Mausolus' name became the root of the word mausoleum, which refers to any stately tomb

The Shrine of the Caaba:

- was located in the Arabian holy city of Mecca
- was revered and preserved on a black stone believed to have been given by an angel to Abraham (also known as Ibrahim)

The Parthenon:

- was the most famous building on the Acropolis of Athens
- served as the "residence of the virgin goddess Athena"
- was designed by the architect Ictinus
- featured sculptures by Phideas

The Pharos was:

- a lighthouse standing at the entrance of the harbor of Alexandria, Egypt
- the first structure of its kind
- built by King Ptolemy to guide the fleets of the world to his capital
- considered to be one of the Seven Wonders of the Ancient World

The Temple of the Seven Spheres was:

- a famous Babylonian temple
- located in the Babylonian suburb of Borsippa
- a huge pyramid, rising 150 feet in seven stages or platforms which were dedicated to the seven planets
- representative of later Babylonian temples
- restored by Nebuchadnezzar II (according to an inscribed cylinder buried beneath its corner)

The Temple of Diana at Ephesus was:

- built during the 6th century B.C.
- considered to be one of the wonders of the world
- burned in the year 356 B.C. by Herostratus (who wanted to immortalize his name), on the same night that Alexander the Great was born
- would have been rebuilt by Alexander if he could have inscribed his name on it (the offer was declined by the Ephesians, who replied that it was not right for one deity to erect a temple to another). They eventually rebuilt it themselves.

The Temple of Vesta was Rome's:

- circular "House of the Vestal Virgins"
- common national hearth, where the sacred fires were kept burning by six mythological virgins considered to be daughters of the Roman state

The Ziggurat of Ur (in present day Iraq) was:

- built by King Ur-Nammu
- dedicated to Nanna (the Sumerian moon goddess).

Thermae:

- were large bath complexes containing chambers for cold, hot, tepid, sudatory, and swimming baths during the time of Imperial Rome
- featured dressing-rooms, gymnasia, museums, libraries, covered colonnades for lounging and conversation, extensive grounds filled with statues and traversed by pleasant walks
- were opened to the public as an exhibition of liberality by their builders

Ziggurats:

- were stepped-tower, early Sumerian temples
- resulted from building each new temple on top of the ruins from the last one
- were named after an Assyrian word meaning pinnacles
- were also built by the Babylonians in honor of their many gods and goddesses

Cultural Artifacts

Sennacherib's Will:

- was found on an Assyrian tabled from the Royal Library at Nineveh
- is probably the oldest will in existence
- conveys personal property to some priests to be held in trust for Sennacherib's sons

The Cap of State:

- was a legendary fur hat decorated with precious metals and jewels first worn by Vladimir II (1053-1125 A.D.), grand prince of Kiev, as a symbol of power
- was worn by later Russian czars (czar, from 'Caesar') inherited and wore the cap

The Rosetta Stone:

- is a heavy block of basalt now housed in a British museum
- because it presents essentially the same text in all three scripts (with some minor differences between them), it provided the key to the modern understanding of Egyptian hieroglyphs.
- is inscribed in demotic, hieroglyphic, and Greek characters

The Stone of Scone:

- was the royal regalia of Scotland
    - carried off to London in 1296 A.D. when Edward I conquered Scotland
- was, as legend had it, the very stone that Jacob used as a pillow in Bethel
- was placed at Westminster Abbey bearing the inscription "Should fate not fail, where'er this stone be found, The Scot shall monarch of that realm be crowned" (a prophecy which was fulfilled when Scotland's James VI became James I of England)

Political Powers and Dynasties

The Amphictyony:

- was an ancient association of Greek tribes formed in the dim past, before the rise of the Greek polis
- was closely connected with religious festivals or rites (e.g. the Delphic Amphictyony was formed to protect the Temple of Apollo at Delphi)

Barracks Emperors:

- were Roman Emperor who seized power by virtue of their command of the army
- met their death by violence (in one stretch, 21 of the 25 emperors who mounted the throne met their end by violence)

Hohenstaufen:

- was a dynasty of German monarchs in the High Middle Ages
- patronized the first pieces of national literature in Germany

The Agora:

- was a general assembly made of up common freemen in Homeric Greece
- was next in power to the council of chiefs
- did not allow its members to vote or participate in debates
- eventually became the popular assembly in the democratic cities of historic Greece

The Constitution of Lycurgus:

- was a system of laws and regulations drawn up by Lycurgus for the Greek city-state Sparta
- was only adopted by the Spartan people after much opposition
- provided for two joint kings, a Senate of Elders, and a Popular Assembly

The College of Pontiffs:

- was named because one of the duties of its members was maintaining the bridges ('pontes') over which religious processions passed
- controlled the calendar (they could lengthen or shorten the year to extend the office of a favorite or to cut short the office of a ruler they disliked)
- called their leader or head "Pontifex Maximus," or the "Chief Bridge-builder" (a title that was later assumed by the Roman emperors and, after them, by the Christian bishops of Rome)

The House of Austria:

- began with the ascension of Duke Albert to the throne (after which the crown of Austria was considered hereditary to the House of Hapsburg)
- continued until Napoleon dissolved the Austrian empire in 1806
- lived in the Castle of Hapsburg in Switzerland, which was called the "cradle of the family"
- always had one of their family members chosen as king by the Electors, though they never went through the formality of an election

Political Powers and Dynasties

Medici:

- was a family that ruled Florence from the 14th to the 18th century A.D.
- controlled one of the largest banking businesses in Europe, from Florence
- were so powerful that they married into many prestigious royal families of Europe
- counted among its members three popes: Leo X, Clement VII, and Leo XI

Pharaohs:

- were kings of Egypt from antiquity
- ruled until Alexander the Great conquered Egypt in 332 B.C.
- derived their name from a word that means "high house"
- have been divided into 31 dynasties
- were viewed as shepherds as well as rulers
- were often depicted as holding a shepherd's crook

Popes (Bishops of Rome)

- became the most important people in Western Europe after the West surrendered to the emperor of the East

Renaissance Papacy:

- referred to the Roman Catholic church government during the Renaissance period
- was interested in spreading its power and influence
- was often opposed to technological advancement or anything that might stimulate thinking

The judges of Israel (such as Gideon, Jepthah, Samson, Eli, and Samuel) were:

- national heroes who led the nation in its early history (before the first king)
- military and/or religious leaders who also performed judicial functions and arbitrated disputes
- were chronicled in the Old Testament book of Judges

Two famous rulers of Babylon were:

- Hammurabi (reigned c. 1795-1750 B.C.)
- Nebuchadnezzar (reigned c. 605-562 B.C.)

The Persian monarchy:

- was a weak one during the final 140 years of the empire's existence
- ended with the reign of Xerxes

The Third Estate (Tiers État)

- was the assembly of the commons in France
- consisted of the Burghers
- was allowed into the feudal assembly in 1302 A.D. by the Capetian king, Philip the Fair

Legislative Bodies

The Tribunal (Council) of the Areopagus:

- was a venerable council held on Areopagus, or Mar's Hill, near the Acropolis
- had its jurisdiction enlarged by Solon
- existed long before democracy was introduced to the Greeks
- was thought to be the tribunal before which the apostle Paul made his eloquent defense of Christianity

The First Triumvirate:

- was a coalition by Caesar, Crassus, and Pompey to seize control of public affairs
- centered on a pledge by each to work for the interests of the others
- had Caesar (the genius of the group) as the ring-leader, Crassus as the wealthy member, and Pompey as the achiever
- resulted in Caesar securing the consulship in 59 B.C.

The Second Diet of Spires:

- took place in 1529 A.D., after the disastrous Peasant's War
- was called to consider the matter of Lutherian Reformers, who had rapidly gained ground
- from this time forward, the reformers began to be known as Protestants – as they were protesting against the abuses of the established church

The Council of Trent:

- played a major role in the Counter Reformation launched by Pope Paul III (in response to the Protestant Reformation)
- met periodically between 1545 and 1563 A.D. to deal with issues raised by the Protestants
- refused to compromise with Protestantism, voting to uphold all Catholic doctrines (including indulgences)
- did institute some changes to reduce the corruption that had been exposed

The House of Commons:

- was formed when Simon de Montfort (a Frenchman in high position) issued writs to plain citizens
- was at first limited to only taking part in tax-related questions
- gradually acquired the right to share in all matters that came before Parliament

The Second Triumvirate:

- consisted of Octavius, Lepidus and Antony
- resulted in the murder of Cicero
- formed 43 B.C.

Legislative Bodies

The Roman Senate:

- was comprised of 300 aristocratic, landowning patricians who were elected for life
- founded c. 753 B.C.
- made the laws for the Roman Republic early in its history
- controlled foreign affairs and selected most government officials
- gradually lost power (later in Roman history, they were simply advisors to the emperor)
- sat next to the elected Roman King
- was composed of the "fathers" and called the "council of old men"
- following the constitutional reforms of the Emperor Diocletian the Senate became politically irrelevant, and never regained the power that it had once held

The Roman consuls (colleagues):

- were a pair of elected patrician magistrates who replaced the king in the Roman Republic
- could each obstruct or veto each other
- were, during times of great danger, superseded in power by an absolute ruler called the "Dictator"

The Roman tribunes:

- consisted of ten elected officials voted into office by the plebeians
- were created to protect plebeians from injustice and shelter them from violence
- had the power to protect plebeians from arrest by patrician magistrates
- protected the plebeians as they struggled for political positions and say in ancient Rome (the plebeians did eventually share power equally with the patricians, and the power struggle between the two classes ceased when Rome became a democracy)

Legal Codes

The Law of Majestas:

- was an old law enforced by the Roman emperor Tiberius
- made it a capital offense to speak or even to think a bad thought about the emperor
- made silence (which could be construed into discontent) equally dangerous
- offered rewards to informers, which led to the emergence of "delators" (people who acted as spies)

The Licinian Laws:

- were enacted around 376 B.C.
- restored the consulship, reserved one of the two consular positions for a plebeian, and introduced new limits on the possession of conquered land
- took the consul's judicial powers and gave them to a magistrate called a praetor
- divided public lands in a more equitable way
- specified that consuls be chosen yearly and that one should be plebeian

The "Code of Hammurabi":

- consisted of 282 case laws which he established
- is based on previous Sumerian laws
- covered family, civil, criminal, and economic laws
- included severe and varied penalties
- considered both the social status of the offender and circumstances of the offence in the prescription of penalties

Legal Codes

The "Body of Civil Law" (Corpus Juris Civilis):

- was published by Tribonian (under the emperor Justinian)
- was one of Rome's great contributions to the legal world
- consisted of three parts: the Code, the Pandects and the Institutes (a fourth part, the *Novellae Constitutiones* was added later)

An Interdict:

- was a papal weapon of banishment that was to a country what excommunication was to an individual
- was used by Pope Innocent III to force Philip Augustus of France to take back his wife after he had put her away
- was also used by Pope Innocent III to force King John of England to appoint Stephen Langton as the archbishop at The See of Canterbury (1199-1216 A.D.)

The Law of the Twelve Tables:

- was drafted by a 10-man board (the decemviri) appointed by the Roman senate in 451 B.C.
- formed the basis of all subsequent Roman private law
- was inscribed on 12 bronze tablets and publicly displayed in the Forum
- was the first systematic codification of Roman law
- included provisions for legal procedure, debt foreclosure, paternal authority, property rights, heirs, and various major and minor offenses
- resulted as part of concessions the patricians made to the plebeians

Systems of Government

A Greek "polis":

- was a city state (such as Athens, Sparta, Corinth, or Thebes)
- became a fundamental and unique institution in Greek society by the 8th century B.C.
- included an "association of kinsmen" made up of the city itself and the surrounding countryside
- resulted from the inability of the Greeks to create a single nation (due to mountainous terrain and island dwellings)
- prohibited its citizens from marrying or holding property in a competing "polis"
- included an:
  - acropolis (hill which served as both a meeting place and a defensive position)
  - agora (an open space which served as marketplace and a place for citizens to assemble)

An Oligarchy:

- is a form of power structure in which power effectively rests with a small number of people
- was preferred by the Dorian cities (The Dorians were one of the four major groups into which the Ancient Greeks of the Classical period considered themselves divided)

A Democracy:

- in its purest or best form would be a society in which all adult citizens have an equal say in the decisions that affect their lives
- was preferred by the Ionian cities (The Ionians were one of the four major groups into which the Ancient Greeks of the Classical period considered themselves divided)

Systems of Government

Feudalism was a Medieval system where:
- a "suzerain, liege, or lord" was granted a "fief" by the king (a "fief was an inheritable piece of land, no matter how small or great)
  - the lord was usually a nobleman such as a baron, knight, etc.
  - the "lord," who was known as the "fiefholder"
    - held the fief for life
    - allowed peasants (vassals) to hold parts of the land in return for labor and a share of the produce
- in theory, all the soil of the country was held by the king as a fief from God
- every holder of a fief became monarch of all he surveyed
- in effect, a descending hierarchy of rights and privileges was granted based on ownership of land
- fiefdoms were conferred by a very solemn ceremony called homage where the person about to become a vassal, serf or "villain":
  - knelt with uncovered head
  - placed his hands in those of his future lord
  - solemnly vowed to be his man from then on, serving him faithfully even until death
- property of a vassal who died without heirs was transferred back to the lord or fiefholder (this was referred to as "By Escheat")
- property that lapsed through disloyalty or another misdemeanor by the vassal was said to be under "forfeiture"
- the lord had the right to demand "aids," or sums of money from his serfs, in order to defray the expense of:
  - knighting his eldest son
  - marrying his oldest daughter, or
  - ransoming himself in case of captivity
- the serfs, who did agricultural work, were not allowed to move from the estate they lived on
- when land was sold, the ownership of the serfs living on it changed hands right along with the buildings
- a 3-tiered societal system existed with:
  - monarchs and clergy at the top
  - the warrior class (knights) in the middle

- - farmers or peasants at the bottom
- craftsmen and merchants were completely ignored, and merchants were scorned, by 11th and 12th century peasants and nobles
- chivalry (the "Flower of Feudalism") was a military institution pledging knights to protect the church, the weak, women, and the oppressed
  - France was the cradle of feudalism
  - the literature of the period is replete with its spirit
  - the Crusades, or Holy Wars (the greatest undertakings of the medieval ages) were predominantly enterprises of the Christian chivalry of Europe
- squires (also known as esquires) became knights at age 21 and were introduced to the order of knighthood by a strange and impressive service where:
  - the knight's arms were given to him
  - his sword was girded on
  - the lord, striking the knight with the flat of his sword on the shoulders or the neck, said, "In the name of God, of St. Michael, and of St. George, I dub thee knight: be brave, bold, and loyal."
- England's legendary King Arthur sat with his Knights of the Round Table, who were bound by oath to help each other in times of danger
  - since the table had no head, all knights were of equal rank
- a war machine (known as the mangonel) used a long, wound-up arm to hurl rocks up to 650 feet
- heavily armored knights, being unrecognizable in war, donned coats of arms to establish identity
  - coats of arms later came to show family membership, alliances, ownership of property, and profession
- gunpowder hastened the downfall of feudalism by making foot soldiers equal in battle to armor-clad knights. Carlyle said of gunpowder, "It made all men of the same height."

Satrapal:

- was a system of government established by Darius the Great
- was emulated by the Turkish Sultan
- featured twenty or more provinces each with a tributary governor (called a satrap) who was appointed (and could be deposed) by the king

Political Offices and Titles

Censors:

- a new type of official set-up by the patricians which could only be filled by a patrician
- instituted in response to the plebeians gaining the right to consulship
- commissioned to watch public morals and, when needed, give wholesome advice
- in place for about a century before plebeians gained the right to be censors as well (in 351 B.C.)

The title "Prince of Wales" was:

- was a title at first assigned to the Welsh chiefs who ruled over an independent Wales
- was last officially held by Llewellyn the Last, who was killed in a war against Edward I in 1282 A.D.
- assumed by Llewellyn's brother
    - Dafydd ap Gruffudd succeeded to the Welsh princeship and issued documents as prince, but was not recognized by the English Crown
- from the death of Llewellyn the Last born by the oldest son of the English monarch

A sibyl:

- was a female Roman orator who prophesied

People

Akkadian

Sargon of Akkad (died 2215 B.C.):

- also known as Sharrukin, was the king of Akkad
- organized the people of the plains and founded the first Mesopotamian empire by uniting Sumer with Akkad
- was called the "Chaldaean Solomon" by the scholar Sayce

Assyrian

Sargon II (died 705 B.C.):

- was the Assyrian king of Ninevah
- began his reign in 722 B.C.
- completed the defeat of the kingdom of Israel by capturing Samaria after a siege of 3 years
- exiled the inhabitants of Samaria from their homeland

Babylonian

Hammurabi (died 1750 B.C.):

- was the 6th king of the Amorite Dynasty of Old Babylon
- was thought to have received the law he became famous for from Shamash, god of justice

Nebuchadnezzar (634-562 B.C.):

- conquered the city of Tyre after a siege of 13 years
- became undisputed ruler over territory stretching from the Zagros Mountains to the Mediterranean
- built the Great Palace in the royal quarter of the city and the famous Hanging Gardens
- engineered a vast irrigation system (including reservoirs and canals) that reached throughout Babylon

Great Britain

Captain James Cook

- (7 November 1728 – 14 February 1779) was a British explorer, navigator and cartographer
- in three voyages sailed thousands of miles across largely uncharted areas of the globe. He mapped lands from New Zealand to Hawaii in the Pacific Ocean in greater detail and on a scale not previously achieved.
- on his third voyage was killed in Hawaii during a fight with the natives

Edward the Confessor (died 1066 A.D.):

- restored the old English line of kings
    - a century-long struggle between the Danes and Anglo-Saxons over control of England had resulted in King Canute of Denmark ruling the English for 25 years
- was deeply religious
- became the object of a religious cult
- was canonized in 1161 A.D. (may have been a strictly political move)

Elizabeth I (1533-1603 A.D.):

- succeeded the Catholic Queen Mary I (Bloody Mary) on the English throne
- was the daughter of Henry VIII's forbidden marriage to Anne Boleyn
    - as a result, she was supported by the Protestants and opposed by the Catholics
- executed the Catholic Mary Queen of Scots for her involvement in plots to assassinate the queen

Edward VI (1537-1553 A.D.):

- was the son of Henry VIII and Jane Seymour
- succeeded Henry VIII to the throne at the age of 9
- died at the age of 15 after reigning only 6 years

Geoffrey Chaucer (1328-1400 A.D.):

- was called the "Father Of English Poetry"
- wrote *Canterbury Tales* (his greatest work) where he represents himself as one of a company of story-telling pilgrims who set out from London on a journey to the tomb of Thomas Becket at Canterbury
- is sometimes credited as the first to show the artistic legitimacy of the English language (rather than French or Latin)

Henry III (1207-1272 A.D):

- was King John's son and successor, becoming king of England
- was taken captive after the Battle of Lewes in 1264 A.D. (though later freed)

Henry VII (1457-1509 A.D.):

- defeated and killed King Richard III, the Earl of Richmond and last of the House of York, in the War of Roses (1455-1485 A.D.)
    - the conflict, which centered around power and place, was so called because both sides had a rose as their badge (the Yorkists, white, the Lancastrians, red)
- was crowned on the battlefield with the diadem which fell from the head of King Richard II
- had been named Henry Tudor, but became known as Henry VII—the first of the Tudors
- wrung money from his wealthy subjects through "benevolences"
    - the wealthy were told that it was very evident they were quite able to make a generous donation to their sovereign
    - those who were financially pinched were told that their economical way of life must have made them wealthy
    - this famous dilemma faced by his subjects became known as "Morton's Fork"

Henry VIII (1497-1547 A.D.):

- was rewarded for his Catholic zeal by Pope Leo X, who conferred the title "Defender of the Faith" upon him in 1521 A.D.
    - Henry VIII retained this title after the Church of England seceded from the Papal See
- became passionately attracted to Anne Boleyn, a beautiful maid in the queen's household
- asked Pope Clement VII for an annulment of his marriage to Catherine so he could marry Anne
- didn't mind annulling his marriage to Catherine and openly breaking with Spain because the Emperor Charles V, to whom Henry VIII had offered the hand of Princess Mary, cast aside the alliance with England by marrying the Infanta of Portugal
- replaced the disgraced Cardinal Wolsey (who failed to procure the desired annulment) with Thomas Cromwell (his own faithful attendant)

- - Cromwell shaped government policy for the next 10 years, executing many who incurred his wrath
- secretly married Anne Boleyn, after which:
  - Parliament passed the Statute of Appeals (making it a crime for Englishmen to take a legal issue out of England to the courts at Rome)
  - Cranmer, a Cambridge doctor who wrote a book in favor of the annulment, was made Archbishop of Canterbury
  - Cranmer declared Henry VIII's marriage to Anne Boleyn to be legal
- was excommunicated by the pope for his marriage to Anne
  - the pope also "relieved" Henry's subjects of their allegiance to Henry
- called Parliament to pass the celebrated "Act of Supremacy" in 1534 A.D., which:
  - made Henry the Supreme Head of the Church of England
  - laid the foundation for the Anglican Church
- executed Sir Thomas More (author of Utopia)
  - lawyer and politician who opposed Protestantism and the abuse of the Church of England, and
  - refused to acknowledge Henry VIII as the Supreme Head of the Church of England
- executed Bishop Fisher, an aged man who also refused to acknowledge Henry VIII as the Supreme Head of the Church of England
- fathered a daughter with Anne Boleyn (who would later become the famous Queen Elizabeth)
- became disillusioned with Anne Boleyn, accused her of unfaithfulness, and had her beheaded
- married Jane Seymour the day after Anne Boleyn's execution
  - Jane died the following year, but did bear him a son named Edward
- took Anne of Cleves as his fourth wife (she was only queen for a few months when Henry became enamored with Catherine Howard)
was asked by Parliament to leave a will, due to the confusion arising from his many divorces

James Stuart VI (1566-1625 A.D.):

- served simultaneously as king of Scotland and England, uniting the crowns in 1603 A.D.
- ended the Scottish independence gained by Robert Bruce at Bannockburn, which the Scotch had maintained for nearly three centuries

John Wycliffe (1328-1384 A.D.):

- was an English theologian, minister and translator
- gave the English people the first complete Bible translation in their native tongue, which
    - had a profound impact on England
- contributed to the start of the Protestant Reformation
- had numerous followers who were derisively called Lollards (babblers), who were
    - precursors of the Protestant Reformation
    - eventually suppressed by force

Mary I (1516-1558 A.D.):

- was a Catholic and the only child of Henry VIII and his ill-fated first wife, Catherine of Arragon
- took the throne after the death of Edward VI (son of Henry VIII and Jane Seymour) died at the age of 15
- killed so many Protestant dissenters during her 5-year reign (280) that she was called "Bloody Mary"
- died without a heir, leaving the throne to her half-sister and rival Elizabeth

Mary, Queen of Scots (1542-1587 A.D.):

- was crowned queen of Scotland when only 9 months old
- fled to England after being suspected in the murder of her husband
- sought the generosity of Elizabeth I but was imprisoned for more than 18 years instead
- conspired (with the Catholics) to assassinate the Protestant Elizabeth 3 different times, which finally led to her execution

Queen Elizabeth (1533-1603 A.D.):

- was the fifth and last monarch of the Tudor dynasty
- found the murder of William of Orange (Prince of Orange) especially alarming, since she knew that the king of Spain had hired agents to kill her as well
- openly embraced the cause of the Dutch in their war for independence from Spain

Richard the Lionheart (1157-1199 A.D.):

- was Richard I, king of England and hero of the Third Crusade
- raised money for the crusade by persecuting the Jews
- reportedly said he would "sell the city of London if he could find a purchaser"
- received a gift of fruit from Saladin, leader of the Arabs, when he was sick during a siege
- received the gift of a fine Arabian steed from Saladin when he lost his horse
- finally agreed to a truce of 3 years and 8 months with Saladin, which allowed Christians free access to the holy places and remain in undisturbed possession of the coast from Jaffa to Tyre

Robin Hood:

- was a heroic outlaw in English folklore
- led the Merry Men and lived in central England's Sherwood Forest
- may or may not have really existed
- was first mentioned in stories in 1377 A.D.

Robert Bruce (1274-1329 A.D.):

- was king of the Scots
- gained Scottish independence by defeating Edward II (of England) in the great battle of Bannockburn (1314 A.D.)
- is memorialized in the poem "King Bruce and the Spider"

Sir Arthur Evans (1851-1941 A.D.):

- was a British archaeologist who believed that the legendary kingdom of King Minos, together with the Minoan civilization of Crete, were real and could be discovered
- used clues from legend to begin the quest to find it
- unearthed the Palace of Minos (now called the Palace of Knossos) in 1900
- reconstructed the incredible Minoan culture, which included indoor plumbing, a peaceful existence, and great palaces whose walls were covered with colorful frescos
- through his excavation, contributed to knowledge of the Aegean Bronze Age

Sir Philip Sidney (1554-1586 A.D.):

- was an English knight and one of the most prominent figures of the Elizabethan Age
- gallantly led British forces into the Netherlands to support the cause of Elizabeth and aid in the revolt against Spain
- was known as the "Flower of Chivalry"
- was mortally wounded at the siege of Zutphen (1586 A.D.)

Sir William Wallace (died 1305 A.D.):

- was a Scottish national hero
- led an army of peasants in a revolt against England
- was quickly betrayed into Edward's hands and condemned to death
- was beheaded in 1305 A.D.
    - his head, garlanded with a laurel crown, was exposed on London Bridge

William the Conqueror (died 1087 A.D.):

- was the first Norman (French) king of England.
- At the battle of Hastings in 1066 A.D. he defeated the English forces led by King Harold Godwinson.
- called a meeting of all tenants of the crown with their vassals
    - required them to take the oath of fealty to him as their feudal lord
    - vassals usually only swore allegiance to their immediate lords
    - greatly reduced the power of the lords or barons by this action
        - broke the bond between vassal and lord

Egyptian

Amenhotep IV:

- was an Egyptian pharaoh
- changed his name to Akhenaten
- was a devout monotheist (believed in only one god)
- prohibited the worship of all gods but Aten, the sun god
- created tremendous religious upheaval in Egypt by smashing the images, excising names, abandoning temples and impounding revenues from gods other than Aten

Khufu I:

- was Cheops to the Greeks
- was a pharaoh in the 4th Egyptian dynasty
- built The Great Pyramid, which is also known as Cheops
- was, like the other "pyramid kings," a great oppressor of the people

Manetho:

- was an Egyptian historian and priest
- lived in the 3rd century B.C.
- compiled a "List of Kings" from manuscripts kept in Egyptian temples
- Divided the Egyptian kings into 30 dynasties (31 are recognized today)

Menes:

- was the first pharaoh of Egypt
- united upper and lower Egypt into a single kingdom
- founded the city of Memphis at the head of the delta of the Nile
- secured Memphis against the river through a vast system of engineering and dikes

Merneptah I (died 1203 B.C.):

- was the 13th son of Rameses II
- reigned only because all of his older brothers predeceased him
- is thought to have been pharaoh during the Israeli Exodus

Necho II (reigned 610-595 B.C.):

- was the last great pharaoh
- commissioned an expedition of Phoenicians to attempt sailing around the continent of Africa (a feat which they reported had been accomplished)
- fought a battle against King Josiah of Israel where Josiah was mortally wounded

Rameses II (1303-1213 B.C.):

- was a 19th Dynasty hero and pharaoh known as Sesostris to the Greeks
- was known by his successors and subjects as "The Great Ancestor"
- is often regarded as the greatest, most famous and powerful pharaoh
- reigned for 67 years
- oppressed the Israelis
- oversaw huge building projects
- fought with the Hittites (though he later married a Hittite princess)
- is depicted in four 70-foot tall statutes in the temple of Ipsambul

The Hyksos (shepherd kings):

- were violent and barbarous Asian conquerors who brought strong, centralized government to Egypt
- spread Egyptian civilization to the Phoenicians and other Mediterranean nations through their business pursuits
- destroyed or mutilated the monuments of Egypt
- were likely in power when the families of Israel found refuge in Lower Egypt (Goshen)

Ethiopian

Queen of Sheba:

- was a famous admirer of King Solomon
- traveled from Ethiopia to witness Solomon's glory
- exclaimed (after viewing Solomon's wisdom and wealth) "the half was not told me."

French

Cardinal Richelieu (1585-1642 A.D.):

- was a French clergyman, nobleman, and statesmen who was the real power during Henry IX's reign in France
- crushed the Huguenots into submission
- stated that "I shall trample all opposition under foot, and then cover all errors with my scarlet robe"
- came to be head of French Affairs when the German "Thirty Year War" was still being fought
  - this war was the last great Protestant / Catholic war in Europe
- gave aid to the Protestant princes of Germany because their success meant the division of Germany and humiliation of Austria

Godfrey of Bouillon (1060-1100 A.D.):

- was a medieval French knight and one of the leaders of the First Crusade
- was crowned "Defender of the Holy Sepulchre" after taking Jerusalem with Tancred as his assistant
- stayed behind with Tancred and a few hundred knights to act as guardians of the holy places

Jean-Francois Champollion (1790-1832 A.D.):

- was the French scholar who decoded the Rosetta Stone
- decoded the hieroglyphic symbols on the stone by comparing the name of Ptolemy, Alexander, and others

Joan of Arc (1412-1431 A.D.):

- is a national hero of France and a Catholic saint
- born a peasant, was known as the Maid of Orleans
- inspired the French coronate Charles at Reims (after the Treaty of Troyes, which promised the French crown to Henry after the death of insane king Charles VI)
- fell into the hands of the English
    - the English burned her at the stake as a heretic and witch
    - her death was a turning point in the 100 Years War, which
        - went steadily against the English after Joan of Arc's death
        - lasted for many more years

Peter the Hermit (died 1115 A.D.):

- was born in Picardy, France
- was commissioned by Pope Urban II to preach a crusade among the masses of Italy and France
- was the immediate cause of the First Crusade
- set out for Constantinople with a mixed throng of about 80,000 people, including women and children
- divided command of his mixed multitude with an impoverished knight, Walter the Penniless
- lost thousands of his followers in battle as they marched, and many more to hunger and exposure
- lost thousands in a slaughter by the Turks
    - the Turks surprised those who did make it across the Bosporous (it would require a trained army of 700,000 knights to finally take Jerusalem in 1099 A.D.)

Greek

Aeschylus (525-456 B.C.):

- was known as the "Father of Tragedy" by the Athenians
- promoted the idea, through his dramas, that "no mortal may dare raise his heart too high" and that "Zeus tames excessive lifting up of heart"
- wrote *Agamemnon*, a great tragedy considered to be his masterpiece

Alexander the Great (356-323 B.C.):

- created one of the greatest empires in the ancient world
- was undefeated in battle and is considered one of history's most successful military commanders
- defeated King Darius of Persia at Arbela
- marched into Babylon without opposition
- seized incredible quantities of gold and silver, the treasure of the Great King, in Susa (up to $57,000,000)
- secured a treasure worth more than twice as much at the defeat of Persepolis ($138,000,000)
- wreaked revenge on Persepolis for all that the Greeks had suffered at the hands of the Persians
- began to see himself as the successor of Darius
- tried to join the Greek and Persian cultures by taking large numbers of Persians into his army and holding a huge ceremony where several thousand of his troops were married to Asian women
- married an Asian princess himself (the daughter of Darius)
- conquered Bactria and Sogdiana (a country lying to the north of Oxus)
- captured and married a Bactrian princess, Roxana
- murdered his own dearest friend, Clitus, after a drunken quarrel (Clitus had once saved Alexander's life, and after the murder, Alexander was filled with remorse)
- conquered King Porus of India after fierce opposition, but spared his life after capture and reinstated him as a vassal, when the

- king responded to Alexander's inquiry about how he should be treated by answering "like a king"
- was seized with a fever, due to his insane excesses, and died at the age of 32 in Babylon

Apelles (4th century B.C.):

- was a renowned painter in ancient Greece and the court painter for Alexander the Great
- was known as the "Raphael of Antiquity"
- insisted that all artists should show their paintings to horses as part of a painting contest where the artists were painting horses
- claimed that when horses saw his painting, they all neighed and exclaimed

Aristophanes (446-386 B.C.):

- was the greatest comic playwright of ancient Athens
- wrote *The Clouds*, *The Knights*, *The Birds*, and *The Wasps* (four of his most noted works that have survived)
- ridiculed the Sophists in his comedy *The Clouds*, and unfairly makes Socrates their representative

Aristotle (384-322 B.C.):

- was a Greek philosopher and polymath (expert in many fields), a student of Plato and teacher of Alexander the Great
- delivered lectures while walking beneath the trees and porticoes of the Lyceum
- profoundly shaped medieval scholarship with his views on physical science, which continued to be influential well into the Renaissance

Codrus (died 1068 B.C.):

- was the last king of Athens
- was killed during the invasion of Attica by Dorians from Peloponnesus

- was dispatched by Spartan soldiers after he disguised himself and attacked them (the Spartans withdrew from the country after learning that the king of Athens was dead)
- was succeeded by a ruler called Archon because no one else was deemed worthy to bear the title of divine king

Demosthenes (385-322 B.C.):

- is widely considered to be one the greatest orators of all time
- failed miserably in his first address to the public assembly, due to defects of voice and manner
- responded by shutting himself up in a cave with the works of Thucydides and shaving one side of his head
- corrected his stuttering by speaking with pebbles in his mouth
- broke the habit of shrugging his shoulders by speaking beneath a suspended sword
- practiced on a noisy seashore to prepare himself for the noise and interruptions of the public assembly
- used his eloquence to stir up the Athenians against the invasions of Philip of Macedon
- is remembered for his famous "Philippics," speeches so fierce that the term came to be used for other writings spewing bitter or violent verbiage

Diogenes (died 323 B.C.):

- was a stoic philosopher who reputedly lived in a tub
- was said to have gone about Athens by daylight with a lantern, in search, he said, of an honest man

Draco (7th century B.C.):

- was the first legislator of Athens in ancient Greece
- crafted a constitution from Athenian customs and regulations, assigning the death penalty to even the smallest offenses
- was the originator of such cruel and "Draconian" laws that it was said that "they were written, not in ink, but in blood"

Epictetus (55-135 A.D.):

- was a Greek sage and Stoic philosopher
- served as a slave in Rome for many years
- was one of the last eminent stoics
    - shared that designation with Marcus Aurelius
    - Christianity brought about the decline of stoicism

Euclid (approx. 3rd century B.C.):

- was a Greek mathematician who lived in Alexandria, Egypt
- was referred to as the "Father of Geometry"
- laid the framework of geometry as still taught today
- wrote *Elements*, one of the most influential works on mathematics used into the late 19th century
- taught King Ptolomy, who disliked the difficulty of Euclid's geometry problems and asked if there was some easier way, to which Euclid replied that "there is no royal road to geometry"

Euripides (480-406 B.C.):

- was one of the three tragic poets of classical Athens, the other two being Aeschylus and Sophocles (Euripides was a more popular dramatist than either)
- wrote more than 90 plays
- was so well-liked by the Sicilians that, according to Plutarch, many of the Athenian prisoners taken by the Syracuse forces during the battle of Sicily, bought their liberty by teaching their masters his verses

Herodotus (484-425 B.C.):

- was an ancient Greek historian known as the "Father of History"
- wrote the legendary four volume series known as *The Histories*
- included *An Account of Egypt*, which gave an accurate eyewitness account of the land and its people, around 456 B.C.
- called Egypt a "gift of the Nile"
- disbelieved the report of Necho II's navigators that they had sailed around the Cape of Africa because they reported that the sun was to their right hand (north) as they rounded the cape (in those days it was believed that the sun went around the earth)
- was an ancient Greek writer, born in Halicarnassus, in Asia Minor
- known as the "Father of History," was the first historian known to collect materials systematically, test their accuracy, and arrange them in a well-constructed and vivid narrative
- traveled over much of the then known world, visiting Italy, Egypt, and Babylonia
- gave a fresh eye-witness account of the wonders he saw

Homer:

- was the earliest Greek poet
- lived at the end of the Mycenaean age
- wrote the Homeric poems, Iliad and Odyssey

Hippocrates was:

- an ancient Greek physician of the Age of Pericles (Classical Athens)
- one of the most outstanding figures in the history of medicine
- considered to be the father of Western medicine

Hypatia (died 415 A.D.):

- was a Greek Neoplatonist philosopher in Roman Egypt and the first notable woman in mathematics
- was beautiful and gifted
- was torn to pieces in A.D. 415 on the streets of Alexandria by fanatical Christian monks

Lysander (died 395 B.C.):

- commanded the Spartan fleet through the Hellespont (a narrow strait), defeating the Athenians at Aegospotami in 405 B.C.
- brought the Peloponnesian War to an end by forcing the Athenians to capitulate
- organized the dominion of Sparta over Greece in the last decade of his life

Pericles (495-429 B.C.):

- was a prominent and influential statesman, orator, and general of Athens during the city's Golden Age
- lived during the time between the Persian and Peloponnesian wars
- made an oration in honor of those who fell in the Peloponnesian Wars, the spirit of which was preserved by the historian Thucydides (who was known for putting speeches into the mouths of his characters)

Phidias (5th century B.C.):

- was a Greek sculptor, painter and architect
- is commonly regarded as one of the greatest of all Classical Greek sculptors

Philip II of Macedon (382-336 B.C.):

- was assassinated while attending the marriage of his daughter in 336 B.C.
- was succeeded by his son, Alexander the Great, who was only 20 years old when he came to the throne

Pindar (522-443 B.C.):

- was an Ancient Greek lyric poet from Thebes
- insisted on virtue and self-culture in his poetry
- wrote of the splendors of the Olympian chariot races and the glory of the victors at other Greek games
- is known for the phrase "become that which thou art"
- was so respected by Alexander the Great that, when the conqueror leveled the city of Thebes in response to a revolt, the house where Pindar had lived 100 years earlier was spared

Plato (424-347 B.C.):

- was a Classical Greek philosopher, mathematician, student of Socrates, and writer
- wrote *The Republic,* which portrays his conception of an ideal state
- was opposed to the republic of Athens
- believed that the ideal state was, in many ways, similar to the feudal system of medieval Europe

Plutarch (46-120 A.D.):

- was a Greek historian, biographer, essayist, and Middle Platonist known primarily for writing *Parallel Lives* and *Moralia*
- was known as "the prince of the ancient biographers"
- contrasted the lives of Greek and Roman statesmen and soldiers with a wealth of anecdotes and illustrations

Polykleitos the Elder (4th and 5th centuries B.C.):

- was an important Classical Greek sculptor from Argos
- was known for his famous bronze statues of athletes
- produced one sculpture of a spear bearer which was so perfect it was known as "the rule"

Polyxena:

- was a princess and the beautiful daughter of Priam, a Trojan
- had a picture painted by her of Polygnotus
- was famous for her beauty and her sufferings
- was said to have carried "in her eyelids the whole history of the Trojan War"

Pythagoras (570-495 B.C.):

- was reputedly the first man to call himself a philosopher
- was an Ionian Greek philosopher, mathematician, and founder of the religious movement called Pythagoreanism
- viewed the solar system as being a "harmony of the spheres," with planets and stars moving according to mathematical equations which corresponded to musical notes, thus producing a symphony
- credited with discovering the Pythagorean theorem (a staple of geometry)

Sappho (died around 570 B.C.):

- was a poet from the island of Lesbos (an Aeolian island that was home to some early poets)
- was thought by the Greeks to be on the same level as Homer
- was called the "Tenth Muse" by Plato
- is still famous, though her poetry (except fragments) has perished

Socrates (469-399 B.C.):

- was a classical Greek Athenian philosopher
- is credited with being a founder of Western philosophy
- is chiefly known through the accounts of his students Plato and Xenophon
- was condemned to die by drinking a fatal dose of hemlock because he had spoken lightly of the Athenian deities
- spent the night before his death discoursing with his students, in "Socratic dialogue," regarding his beliefs on immortality of the soul

Solon (638-558 B.C.):

- was a Greek lawmaker who laid the foundation for Athenian democracy
- repealed many of Draco's cruel "Draconian" laws
- permitted exiled persons to return
- helped debtors (especially poor farmers) by freeing those held in slavery for debt and cancelling all fines payable to the state
- created contentment and prosperity throughout Attica due to his policies

Thucydides (460-395 B.C.):

- was the Greek historian who write the book *History of the Peloponnesian War*
- argued that the war resulted due to an imbalance of power between Athens and Sparta and the fear that Athens inspired
- believed that war was inevitable due to the growth and insatiable demand for expansion of the Athenian empire

Zeno (333-264 B.C.):

- founded the Stoic school of philosophy
- taught at a public porch in Athens (which was called a "stoa," leading his followers—who sat on the porch—to be called "stoics")

Israelite

King David (1040-970 B.C.):

- was the second king of the Hebrew (Israelite) nation
- transformed the pastoral and half-civilized Israeli tribes into a conquering people
- extended the limits of his empire in every direction
- waged successful wars against the nations of Moab and Edom

King Jeroboam (died 901 B.C.):

- ruled 10 of the 12 tribes of Israel after the reign of Solomon (when all the tribes except Benjamin and Judah revolted)
- ruled the northern kingdom of Israel (the southern state was the rival Kingdom of Judah)

King Saul (1079-1007 B.C.):

- was the first king of the Hebrew (Israelite) nation
- suffered from depression and insanity near the end of his reign
- fell in battle with three of his sons on Mount Gilboa

King Solomon:

- was the youngest son of King David and succeeded him on the throne
- erected the "Temple of Solomon" which his father had planned for Jerusalem (the capital city)
- was considered the wisest man who ever lived
- became an idolater
- had 700 wives and 300 concubines

Persian

Artaxerxes II (died 358 B.C.):

- was known to be called Mnemon due to his remarkable memory (today a mnemonic device is any learning technique that aids memory)
- survived an attempt to wrest the throne led by his brother (Cyrus the Younger) known as the expedition of Ten Thousand Greeks (the uprising ended when Cyrus the Younger was killed)
- may have been the king who was married to the biblical Queen Esther

Cyrus II (died 530 B.C.):

- was commonly known as Cyrus the Great
- led the Persian revolt against the Medes
- built a colossal empire
- planned to burn Croesus (a captured Lydian king) on a funeral pyre
- spared Croesus after hearing him repeat the name of the philosopher "Solon" three times while on the funeral pyre (Solon had told Croesus, during happier times, to "count no man happy until he is dead")

Darius the Great (550-486 B.C.):

- was also known as Darius I
- has been called "the second founder of the Persian Empire"
- built canals, underground waterways, a powerful navy, and a network of post roads throughout his dominion
- instituted coinage for his realm
- inscribed a record of his achievements on the great rock of Behistun
- conquered Punjab (the northwest region of India), Babylonia, Thrace, and Macedonia—which vastly increased his tributary revenues in addition to expanding his borders
- used pontoon bridges (constructed by Greek architects) to cross the Bosphorous and the Danube, penetrating far into what is now Russia and gaining Persia's first foothold on the European continent

Roman

Julius Caesar (100-44 B.C.):

- was a Roman general, statesman, and distinguished writer of Latin prose who played a critical role in the gradual transformation of the Roman Republic into the Roman Empire
- overthrew Ptolemy while in Egypt
- accumulated more absolute and unrivaled power than any consul in Roman history
- secured Egypt for Cleopatra and her younger brother
- fathered a son with Cleopatra
- declined Mark Antony's offer to coronate him several times, due to the displeasure of those who heard it
- was assassinated on the Ides (15th day) of March in 44 B.C. by 70-80 conspirators in the Senate, let by Cassius and Brutus
- had been forewarned of an assassination attempt by Spirinna, an astrologer
- exclaimed "Et tu, Brute," which means "Even you, Brutus?" when Brutus raised his dagger
- did not resist the 23 stabs that killed him

Caligula (12-41 A.D.):

- was also known as Gaius Caesar
- succeeded Tiberius as emperor of Rome when only 25 years old
- was even more cruel than Tiberius, stating at one time that he wished that "the people of Rome had but one neck"
- insulted his nobles by proposing to make his favorite horse, Incitatus, consul
- declared himself to be divine
- removed the heads of Jupiter's statues, replacing them with his own likeness

Claudius (10-54 A.D.):

- completed "The Claudian Aqueduct"
    - an incredible system which brought water to Rome from 45 miles away
    - it failed after 10 years of use and wasn't repaired until 9 years later, by Vespasian
- married the "wicked Agrippina" as his fourth wife
    - she was reputed to have murdered him with poisonous mushrooms so that her son, Nero, could take the throne

Camillus (446-365 B.C.):

- was a Roman soldier, statesman, and dictator of patrician descent
- conquered the city of Veii in 396 B.C. (the richest city of the Etruscan League, located about 10 miles from Rome)

Cicero (106-43 B.C.):

- was a famous Roman statesman and orator
- exposed an internal conspiracy by Catiline and other nobleman in his famous Philippic, "The First Oration Against Catiline"
    - Catiline fled as a result of Cicero's oration, was killed in a battle near Pistoria, and his head was taken as a trophy to Rome
- was hailed as the "Savior of his Country" for exposing Catiline

People

Cincinnatus (520-430 B.C.):

- was a patrician farmer and one of the first Roman dictators
- was appointed ruler for six months during the Aequian siege of Rome
- raised up an army, captured the entire enemy force, then gave up his office and returned to his farm

Commodus (161-191 A.D.):

- was the son Marcus Aurelius and succeeded him as emperor of Rome
- co-ruled with Marcus Aurelius during the last years of his reign
- was a "Barracks Emperor"
    - a string of emperors who were elected by the army
        - 21 of the 25 met their deaths by violence

Constantine (272-337 A.D.):

- was the first Christian emperor of the Roman world
- made Christianity the state religion in 313 A.D. with a decree known as the Edict of Milan (the edict, which was signed by Constantine and Lincinius, also extended toleration to Christians and restored any property that had been confiscated during the persecution)
- continued to tolerate other forms of worship
- was converted when, during a military campaign, he reputedly saw a luminous cross in the sky with the inscription "with this sign you will conquer"
- made the cross the royal standard—under his leadership, Roman legions marched beneath the emblem of Christianity for the first time
- subsidized the Christian church from public funds
- exempted the clergy from public obligations
- set the religious tone for future Roman emperors, all of whom were Christians except for Julian (360-363 A.D.), who attempted to restore the polytheistic religions
- selected Byzantium as the new capital of the Roman empire and changed its name to Constantinople

- issued the first imperial edict against the sport of gladiators, in 325 A.D. (although the sport wasn't permanently discontinued until decades later)

Crassus (115-53 B.C.):

- was a Roman general, politician, wealthy man and Caesar's staunchest friend
- led an army against the Parthians in an attempt to rival Caesar's Gallic conquests
- was badly defeated
- was executed by his captors, who poured molten gold down his throat to give him more of the metal he had so coveted during his life

Didius Julianus (133-193 A.D.):

- wealthy senator who bought the emperorship from the Praetorian soldiers, who offered to sell it to the highest bidder
- paid $1000 to each of the 12,000 soldiers who composed the guard at the time of the auction
    - a total of $12,000,000
- was ousted within three months by his successor (Septimius Severus), who was angry that he had "bought" the throne

Diocletian (244-311 A.D):

- was a Roman emperor and military commander noted for changes he made in the Roman government
- was equally famous for the cruel persecution he ordered against the Christians
    - the 10th, and most severe, persecution of Christianity took place from A.D. 303 to 311
    - outlawed and hunted all Christians, throwing all who were caught either to wild beasts or into the fire

Julian the Apostate (332-363 A.D.):

- ruled the Roman empire from 360-363 A.D.
- was the only Roman emperor after Constantine who was not a Christian
- labored to restore the pagan and polytheistic religions
- avoided violence against the Christians, resorting to sophistry and ridicule instead
- attempted to rebuild the temple at Jerusalem (contrary to Christian prophecy)
- was thwarted in his attempt to rebuild the Jerusalem temple by gaseous explosions that Christians called a miracle
  - modern analysts suggest explosions due to gas trapped in passages underground

Justinian (482-565 A.D.):

- commonly known as Justinian the Great, was Byzantine Emperor from 527 to 565. During his reign, Justinian sought to revive the Empire's greatness and reconquer the lost western half of the classical Roman Empire.
- best known for reforming and codifying Roman law
  - his legal code still forms the basis of many legal systems in Europe today

Fabius Maximus (280-203 B.C.):

- was the dictator of Rome who faced Hannibal's siege
- realized that the only prudent choice was avoiding war with Hannibal
- was known as the "Delayer"

Gaius Octavius (100-59 B.C.):

- was a grand nephew of Julius Caesar
- was named in Caesar's will as his heir and successor
- opposed Mark Antony's dictatorship

Marcus Aurelius (121-180 A.D.):

- was the last of the "Five Good Emperors"
- came to the throne in 161 A.D.
- was one of the two last eminent "Stoics" (Epictetus being the other)
- was called a "philosopher" due to his studious habits
- wrote the Stoic book *Meditations*
    - made the nearest approach to the spirit of Christianity of ancient pagan writings
    - is still revered as a monument to the philosophy of service and duty
- fought a war with Parthia that brought back the Asiatic Plague, which decimated entire city populations in Italy
- blamed Christians for the plague and permitted a terrible persecution
    - the famous Christians Justin Martyr and Polycarp were killed during that persecution

Marcus Manlius (died 384 B.C.):

- was a patrician who saved the city of Rome from the Gauls
- was later executed for helping the plebeians

Mark Antony (83-30 B.C.):

- was a Roman politician, military commander, and loyal friend of Julius Caesar
- betrayed his faithful wife Octavia for the beautiful Cleopatra
- planned to make Alexandria the capital of the Roman world
- wanted to make Caesarion (son of Caesar and Cleopatra) heir of the empire
- fled for his life after losing the Battle of Actium, with Octavius in pursuit
- heard a false report that Cleopatra was dead and committed suicide (Cleopatra then tried to seduce Octavius, but failing in this pursuit, also committed suicide)

Nero (37-68 A.D.):

- persecuted the Christians on a grand scale
- was in the 10th year of his reign as emperor when t... .... of Rome burned through more than half of the city
- may have ordered the fire to be lit (he enjoyed watching it from the roof of his palace)
- amused himself during the fire by singing a poem he composed entitled "Sack of Troy"
- was driven from the throne in 68 A.D. and facing assassination committed suicide soon after

Octavius (63-14 A.D.):

- was also known as Augustus
- lived for 76 years and reigned for 44 (from 31 B.C. to 14 A.D.)
- ruled during a splendid period Rome's history (referred to as the Pax Romana)
- was able to keep order on the frontiers of his empire while enjoying no real opposition at home
- brought peace and prosperity that would last two centuries during his reign
- was accorded divine worship by the Senate after his death
    - temples were erected in his honor
    - it was believed that his soul ascended visibly from the flames of his funeral pyre

Pliny the Elder (23-79 A.D.):

- was a Roman author, naturalist and natural philosopher, as well as naval and army commander of the early Roman Empire, and personal friend of the emperor Vespasian
- died because he ventured too close to the volcano Vesuvius while it erupted
    - the cities of Pompeii and Herculaneum were buried during that eruption

Pompey (106-48 B.C.):

- was a military and political leader of the Roman Republic
- subdued the pirates in the Mediterranean sea (66 B.C.)
- defeated Mithridates the Great, Syria, Phoenicia, Coele-Syria, and Palestine
- paraded 322 captive princes in front of his chariot upon his homecoming to Rome
- proclaimed (through banners) that he had conquered 21 kings, 1000 strongholds, 900 towns, 800 ships, and more than 12,000,000 people

Romulus (born 771 B.C.):

- was the first Roman king
- was often considered to be the sole founder of Rome
- may have founded Rome with his twin brother, Remus

Servius Tullius (died 535 B.C.):

- was the 2nd king of the Etruscan dynasty
- drained a large tract of marshy land by means of the Cloaca Maxima, the "Great Sewer," to create a place for the "Forum" (a gathering place for the people)
- made an important change in Roman law by making property, rather than birth, the basis of the constitution (just as his counterpart Solon was doing in Athens)
- divided the Roman population into five classes
    o the first or highest class owned at least twenty jugera (about twelve acres of land)
    o the fifth or lowest class included all who owned at least two jugera (about 1 acre)

St. Augustine (354-430 A.D.):

- was also known as Augustine of Hippo
- was a Latin philosopher and theologian from Roman Africa
    - his writings were very influential in the development of Western Christianity
- wrote in Latin (like all church fathers during his time)
- penned *City of God*
    - asserted that secular government and authority were necessary for the pursuit of the true Christian life on Earth
- taught predestination
    - the concept that some people are "predestined" to receive salvation
        - later greatly influenced such theologians as Thomas Aquinas and John Wesley
- provided one of the best examples (through his works) of how Christian theologians used pagan culture to promote Christianity

Sulla (138-78 B.C.):

- was a Roman general and statesman who had the rare distinction of holding the office of consul twice, as well as that of dictator
- sent Marius into exile after defeating him in a civil war
    - Marius later recaptured Rome and killed many of Sulla's supporters before dying in 86 B.C. at the age of 71 while Sulla was away
- returned to Rome for revenge, although a fire at Capitol Hill that burned up the Sibylline Books was believed to foreshadow doom
- slaughtered the poor by thousands, as well as many of the nobles, upon his return
- declared himself dictator for life, but retired after 3 years and died

Tacitus (56-117 A.D.):

- was a senator and historian of the Roman empire
- penned *Germania* (his most famous work)
    - a treatise on the manners and customs of the Germans
    - exalted the simple life of uncivilized Germans
    - contrasted German virtue with the immoralities of the refined and cultured Romans

Tarquin the Proud (535-496 B.C.):

- was the legendary last king of Rome (also known as Tarquinius Superbus)
- an arbitrary tyrant so horrible that patricians and plebeians united to drive him into exile in 509 B.C.
    - this Roman tyrant was expelled just one year after the expulsion of the Athenian tyrants

Tiberius (42 B.C.-37 A.D.)

- was emperor of Rome when:
    - Christ was crucified
    - the followers of Jesus traversed the empire, preaching the "glad tidings" everywhere
    - the empire began its transition from pagan to Christian

Titus (39-81 A.D.):

- was a Roman emperor and the son of Vespasian (the emperor he succeeded)
- conquered Jerusalem after one of the longest sieges in history
- destroyed the Jewish temple
- killed more than a million Jews, many by crucifixion

Titus Lucretius Carus (99-55 B.C.):

- was a Roman poet and philosopher
- believed in evolution
- wrote a famous poem, *On the Nature of Things*, which
    - anticipated many of the conclusions of modern scientists
    - discussed the axiom of nothing, which deals with the atomic nature of the universe, theories regarding the senses, natural phenomena, and disease

Verres (120-43 B.C.):

- was a Roman magistrate and scoundrel notorious for his misgovernment of Sicily
- prosecuted by Cicero (who was rising into prominence as a brilliant orator in Rome just at that time)
- fled to Massilia due to the storm of indignation raised by the trial, taking with him much of his ill-gotten wealth

Zeno (425-491 A.D):

- was Byzantine emperor during the 5th century A.D.
- ruled Constantinople
- reigned when the Roman empire fell in the west (476 A.D.)
    - a German chief was set-up as patrician in Italy
    - Rome became a province under him

Enemies of Rome

Alaric I (370-410 A.D.):

- was King of the Visigoths from 395–410 A.D.
- is best known for his plunder of Rome in 410 A.D.
    - was a decisive event in the decline of the Roman Empire
    - led pagans to abandon their faith and give credence to Christian prophecies of Apocalypse
- died shortly after sacking Rome

Antiochus III the Great (of Syria)(241-187 B.C.):

- ruled over greater Syria and western Asia in the 3rd century B.C.
- was defeated by Scipio, brother of Africanus (who changed his name to Asiaticus after the victory)
- was overthrown after the Romans defeated him in the Battle of Magnesia (190 B.C.)
    - as a result, much of Asia Minor was conquered by Rome

Atilla the Hun (died 453 A.D.):

- ruled the Huns and their empire
- was one of the most feared enemies of the Western and Eastern Roman Empires
- was known as the "Scourge of God"
    - a warrior so fierce that the grass never grew again "where once the hoof of Attila's horse had trod"
- retreated after the Battle of Chalons (451 A.D.)

Hannibal (287-183 B.C.):

- was a was a brilliant Phoenician/ Carthaginian military commander and tactician
- was once called "the foremost man of his race and his time, perhaps the mightiest military genius of any race and of any time."
- reignited the war between Rome and Carthage by laying siege to Saguntum (a city protected by Rome) in 219 B.C.
- surprised the Romans with a lightning march from Spain over the Pyrenees and the Alps into Italy
- incorrectly believed that Rome's Italian allies would defect in hordes after Rome lost several battles
- inflicted several defeats on the Romans during the Second Punic War, including:
    - a monumental victory at Cannae where the Romans suffered about 70,000 casualties
    - advanced within sight of Rome, and might have taken the city if Rome had not been rescued by its Italian allies

- returned to Carthage after losing the war, then fled first to Syria, then Asia Minor, to escape the Romans
- poisoned himself in 183 B.C. to avoid being turned over to the Romans
    - repelled by a combined Gothic-Roman army

Spartacus (109-71 B.C.):

- was a famous leader of the slaves in the Third Servile War, a major slave uprising against the Roman Republic
- was from Thrace (in southeastern Europe)
- established a stronghold of slaves, gladiators and discontents at Vesuvias while Gnaeus Pompey was away to put down a Marian revolt in Spain
- was eventually killed in battle with the Romans, who punished the survivors of his army with typical Roman cruelty

The Franks

Charlemagne (742-814 A.D.):

- was the son of Pepin the Short, also known as Charles
- is regarded as the founding father of both French and German monarchies, and the "Father of Europe"
- launched 52 military campaigns in his 46 years as king
- once had the rear of his army plundered in a mountain pass by Gascon and Basque mountaineers and could not help them. This incident:
    - was the favorite theme of the Troubadours of South France
    - gave rise to the Song of Roland, based on the faithful martyr officer Count Hruoland
- punished Pope Leo III's opposition (they were exiled)
    - received as a reward the pope's declaration that he was king of Byzantine
- was crowned emperor of Rome by the pope in 800 A.D., marking the birth of the "Holy Roman Empire"

- died in 814 A.D., after which his giant empire disintegrated and was divided among his children according to the Treaty of Verdun:
    - The treaty effectively created the three great nations of modern Europe: France, Italy, and Germany
        - Charles the Bald was given France
        - Lewis was given Germany, and
        - Lothair was given Italy and the valley of the Rhone, together with a narrow strip of land extending from Switzerland to the mouth of the Rhine

Duke Charles Martel (686-741 A.D.):

- was a Frankish political and military leader
- led the Franks at the Battle of Tours in 732 A.D.
    - crushed the Saracens (Arabs) and stopped them from over running Europe
    - forced them to retreat beyond the Pyrenees
- was also known as "Charles the Hammer" or "Martel the Hammer"
    - due to the mighty blows of his huge battle-axe

Pepin the Short (died 768 A.D.):

- was king of the Franks and Duke Charles Martel's son
- crowned himself king with the consent of Pope Stephen II
    - unlike his father who was king only in authority, not in name
- returned Pope Stephen II's favor by driving out the Lombards and giving those lands to the papacy, which gave rise to papal states
- was succeeded by Carloman, who died shortly after taking the throne

Leaders of Islam

Abubekr (573-634 A.D.):

- succeeded the Muslim prophet Muhammad
- assumed the title of Caliph, or Vicar of the Prophet
- was not accepted in this position by all Muslims
    - many thought Ali (Muhammad's cousin and son-in-law) should be the successor
    - this disagreement eventually divided Islam into two rival sects

Caliph Omar (586-644 A.D.):

- was a leading companion and adviser to Muhammad
- was also known as Umar
- succeeded Abubekr (who had succeeded Muhammad)
- led the Islamic invasion into North Africa
- burned the entire library of Alexandria, saying "If these books agree with the Koran, they are useless; if they disagree, they are pernicious: in either case they ought to be destroyed."

Muhammad (570-632 A.D.):

- was the great prophet of the Arabs who founded the religion of Islam
- was born in the city of Mecca and spent much of his life as a shepherd
- came from the distinguished tribe of the Koreishites
    - custodians of the sacred shrine of the Caaba
- claimed to have visions while meditating in a cave near Mecca
- said the angel Gabriel appeared to reveal what he should make know to his fellow man, which, in summary, was "There is but one God (Allah), and Muhammad, is his Prophet"
- is believed by the Muslims to be the last and greatest of the four great prophets—greater than Moses, David, or Jesus
- escaped an assassination attempt by angry Koreishites
- fled to Medina in 622 A.D.
    - the word Hegira refers to this flight

- Muslims considered it as start of an era and reckoned their dates from that time

Russia

Ivan the Great (1462-1505 A.D.):

- reorganized Russia, making Moscow (Muscovy) its capital city
- freed Russia from the hateful Tartar domination
- consolidated the Russian monarchy

Vladimir I (956-1015 A.D):

- was grand prince of Russia's Kiev and Novgorod
- concluded that his state needed a major religion
- sent envoys to investigate Islam, Judaism, Roman and Byzantine Christianity
- was won over by the news of a mass in Sophia Cathedral in Constantinople, which resulted in the start of the Russian Orthodox Church
- agreed to marry Anna, sister of Byzantine emperor Basil II

Poland

Boleslaw the Brave (967-1025 A.D.):

- was the first king of Poland
- reigned for only a short time, from 1024-1025 A.D.
- reorganized the church in Poland, making it responsible to the pope
- united Poland with his military campaigns
  - it disintegrated into factions again after his death

Casimir the Great (1310-1370 A.D.):

- was a Polish king who:
    - extended Polish territory and encouraged learning
    - united Poland into one country
    - ruled in the 14th century

Wenceslaus (1316-1378 A.D.):

- was also known as Charles IV
- was the second king of Bohemia (a region in the west of the present day Czech Republic)
- was the first king of Bohemia to be crowned the "Holy Roman Emperor"
- became the patron saint of the country after his death
- made Prague his capital city
- founded the Charles University in 1348 A.D.

Christian

Francis Xavier (1506-1552 A.D.):

- was a Catholic missionary born in the Kingdom of Navarre (currently Spain)
- was known as the "Apostle of the Indies"
- one of the most distinguished of the Jesuit missionaries to serve in pagan lands
- the first Jesuit to go to Japan as a missionary

John Calvin (1509-1564 A.D.):

- was an influential French theologian and pastor during the Protestant Reformation
- fled France and found refuge in Geneva due to religious persecution
- consented to the burning of Servetus (1553 A.D.) because he thought his teachings were heretical
- taught the concept of election or predestination, which held that:

- a select, predestined group of people would go to heaven based on God's choice
- nothing we do can change who will or will not go

Martin Luther (1483-1546 A.D.):

- was an Augustine monk and a teacher of theology in the university of Wittenberg
- visited Rome in 1510 A.D. and found himself shocked at the greed and worldliness of Roman clergy
- was especially upset by the Roman Catholic practice of selling indulgences
  - indulgences were used to finance large building projects people were told they could buy God's forgiveness by giving
- was foremost among those who opposed and denounced Tetzel (the papal emissary who selling indulgences, or pardons for sin)
- drew his famous 95 Theses in 1517 A.D., in which he strongly denounced church corruption and the practice of selling indulgences
- nailed the 95 Theses, written in Latin, to the door of the Wittenberg church
- was recipient of a "papal bull" (1520 A.D.) issued by Pope Leo X
  - the bull declared Martin Luther a heretic and banned all his writings
- publicly burned the papal bull at the gates of Wittenberg
- was summoned by Charles V to face the Diet of Worms (an assembly of princes, nobles, and clergy of Germany) which:
  - declared him a heretic and an outlaw, but
  - allowed him to leave safely
  - on the way home was intercepted by masked men (friends) and escorted to Wartburg castle
- stayed in the castle of his friend Frederick the Wise, who kept him there for safety while he worked on his famous translation of the Bible

Pope Alexander VI (1451-1503 A.D.):

- was one of the most controversial of the Renaissance popes
- tried to solve the territorial conflict between Spain and Portugal by dividing the world
    - drew a meridian line about midway through the Atlantic after the return of Columbus
    - gave all unclaimed pagan lands west of the line to Spain, and those east of the line to Portugal

Pope Gregory VII (died 1085 A.D.):

- was pope at a time when the Roman church possessed half of the lands in Europe
- was also known as Hildebrand
- suppressed the evil of simony (the act of paying money for sacraments and sacred offices)
- introduced celibacy for the Roman clergy (from 1073-1080 A.D.)
- had his reforms strongly opposed by Henry IV of Germany and the Hohenstaufen dynasty
    - this was simply the continuation of the power struggle about who should be first, the "world priest" or the "world king, a contest which ended with the final triumph of the Roman bishops and the ruin of the Hohenstaufen

Pope John XXII (1244-1344 A.D.):

- was the second pope of the Avignon Papacy
    - the Avignon Papacy was a line of seven popes who ruled from Avignon, France
- excommunicated the Holy Emperor Ludwig IV (Louis IV) of Bavaria in 1324 A.D.
    - Ludwig retaliated four years later by setting up an anti-pope in Rome

Pope Leo X (1475-1521 A.D.):

- found the coffers of the Catholic church almost empty when he was elected as pope in 1513 A.D.
- offered a grant of indulgences to raise money for his various undertakings, including
  - work on St. Peter's Basilica
  - Michelangelo's work

Pope Nicholas V (1397-1455 A.D.):

- generously promoted the humanistic movement
- served as pope from 1447-1455 A.D.
- established the Vatican library

Tetzel (1465-1519 A.D.):

- was a Dominican friar employed by the Archbishop of Magdeburg, and ultimately by Pope Leo X, to dispense indulgences as his deputy in Saxony
- convinced people that if they contributed to the building of St. Peter's at Rome they would be exempt from all penalty for sins
- was denounced by protesters, including (and foremost) among whom was Martin Luther (the great Protestant reformer)

Spanish

Rodrigo Diaz de Vivar (1043-1099 A.D.):

- was a Castilian (Spanish) nobleman, military leader, and diplomat
- was better known as el Cid, or "the chief"
- had served the king of Castile in Spain
- was banished from court by Spanish emperor Alphonso VI after being wrongly accused of disloyalty
- gathered a small army in 1094 A.D. and defeated the Moors to conquer Valencia

People

Asian

Genghis Khan (died 1227 A.D.):

- founded the great Mongol empire of Asia and Europe, conquering most of Eurasia
- was known as the "Universal Sovereign"
- his military campaigns were often accompanied by wholesale massacres of civilian populations and is responsible for slaughtering as many as 40 million people during his lifetime

Tamerlane (1336-1405 A.D.):

- was also known as Timour the Lame
- was a 14th-century conqueror of West, South and Central Asia
- succeeded Ghengis Khan and re-consolidated the Mongol empire
    - fragments of his empire later became the Moghul dynasty in Delhi and Agra in India
- checked the power of the Turks in the Battle of Angora
    - forced the Turks to lift the siege on Constantinople

Other Leaders of Europe

Canute (died 1035 A.D.):

- was a king of Denmark who ruled over England for 25 years
- according to legend, Canute's courtiers made him believe that his word was so powerful as to even control the ocean tide. He reportedly set his throne near the shore and almost drowned while ordering the tide to recede

Empress Irene (752-803 A.D.):

- a Byzantine empress who deposed her own son (Constantine VI) from the throne
    - even took out his eyes
- could not rule herself since the crown of the Caesars could not be worn by a woman
- opened the door for Charlemagne

Frederick Barbarossa (1152-1190 A.D.)

- was the most noted ruler of the Hohenstaufen line in Germany
- was recognized by his red beard
- died in the Third Crusade
- was hero of a legend that said
    - he slept in a cavern beneath one of his castles on a mountain-top
    - when the ravens should cease to circle about the hill he would appear to make the German people a united and strong nation

Gustavus Vasa (1496-1560 A.D.):

- was a Swedish nobleman
- led a revolt that helped the Swedes regain their independence in 1523 A.D.
- ruled as King of Sweden from 1523 A.D. until his death

Ludwig IV (1282-1347 A.D):

- was king of Bavaria, also known as Ludwig IV
- was a Holy Roman Emperor
- was excommunicated by Pope John XXII in 1324 A.D.
- set-up an anti-pope in Rome in retaliation four years later

People

Margaret I of Denmark (1353-1412 A.D.):

- ruled Denmark, Norway, and Sweden
- was founder of the Kalmar Union (1397 A.D.), which united the Scandinavian countries under one crown for more than a century
- because of her political prowess was known as the "Semiramis of the North"

Otto the Great (912-973 A.D.):

- was the first of the Germans to be called emperor of Italy
- restored the fallen Roman imperial power in the middle of the 10th century
    - it became known as the Holy Roman Empire
- effectively created a power to compete with the papacy, thereby igniting the struggle for supremacy between the "Holy Roman Empire" and the papacy

Roger II (1095-1154 A.D.):

- conquered Sicily and became its first Norman king
- came to power in the 11th century, 6 years after the Normans invaded England
- fostered a court that was an important center for both Christian and Muslim scholars
- started the trend that, by the end of the 12th century, led to Sicily being the most advanced state in Europe

Stefan Dusan (1308-1355 A.D.):

- was a Serbian king, also emperor of the Serbs and Greeks
- fought successfully against the Byzantine empire (although the country broke up after his death)

Stefan Nemanja (1113-1199 A.D.):

- was a prince of Serbia, best remembered for his contributions to culture and history
- united Serbia (for the first time) late in the 12th century

Suleiman the Magnificent (1494-1566 A.D.):

- was tenth and longest reigning Sultan of the Ottoman Empire
- forged an alliance with Francis I of France in the Third War against Charles V
    - the alliance which shocked all Christendom
- ravaged the Italian coast with his fleet
- sold his plunder and captives in the port of Marseilles

William of Orange (1533-1584 A.D.):

- was chief leader of the Dutch revolt against the Spanish that set off the Eighty Years' War and resulted in the formal independence of the Netherlands
- earned the title "the Founder of Dutch Liberties," and was also known as the "Prince of Orange"
- was banned and declared an outlaw by Philip II, who offered an assassin's reward that included pardon for all sins, a title of nobility, and 25,000 gold crowns
- was fatally shot by an assassin

Painters, Poets and Writers (Renaissance)

Dante Alighieri (1265-1321 A.D.):

- was a great Florentine poet who often wrote love-letters to his favorite authors
- is best known for his *Divine Comedy*, which is considered to be the "Epic of Medievalism"
- wrote a love letter to Homer lamenting the lack of taste among his countrymen and declaring that not more than 10% of Italians could appreciate the *Iliad*

Donatello (1386-1466 A.D.):

- sculpted the first free-standing sculpture since ancient times
- called it *David* and placed it in the *Palazzo Vecchio*
    - this is not the same as Michelangelo's well-known sculpture of David

Filippo Brunelleschi (1377-1446 A.D.)

- designed and built the double-shelled dome of Florence Cathedral from 1418-1436 A.D.
- is considered the founder of Renaissance architecture

Froissart (1337-1405 A.D.):

- was, with his skilled and entertaining storytelling style, the first noted writer of French prose
- was one of the most important historians of medieval France, known as the French Herodotus
- provided an important source of information regarding the first half of the 100 Years War

Giotto (1266-1337 A.D.):

- was the painter of The Kiss of *Judas* (1306 A.D.) to whom the anecdote of drawing the "perfect circle" is often attributed
- was a revolutionary who altered the course of painting in Western Europe
- moved away from the Gothic and Byzantine styles and more towards the Renaissance
- was put in charge of public works in Florence in 1334 A.D.

Giovanni Boccaccio (1313-1375 A.D.):

- was a notable Italian author who wrote the first modern novel in 1353 A.D.
- included 100 raucous stories in that novel, entitled *Decameron* which:
    o described the Black Death plague (which had just concluded)
    o introduced 7 ladies and 3 young men who gathered in a villa near Naples to escape the plague, and who tell each other stories to pass the time

Leonardo da Vinci:

- was a famed painter, sculptor, architect, and engineer
- has been described as the model Renaissance Man—one with unquenchable curiosity and feverishly inventive imagination
- produced very few paintings (only 17 survive, and of that number, several are unfinished)
- painted *The Last Supper* and *Mona Lisa* (his most renowned)

Leone Batista Alberti (1404-1472 A.D.)

- was a brilliant humanist, architect, painter and philosopher
- made one of the greatest contributions to the Renaissance through his publication of his art treatise entitled *Della Pittura*
- was intrigued by the work of architect Filippo Brunelleschi
    o dedicated his famous study in which one finds everything known about perspective to Brunelleschi

Painters, Poets and Writers (Renaissance)

Michelangelo (1475-1564 A.D.):

- is an Italian artist who exerted an unparalleled influence on the development of Western art
- is considered one of the greatest artists of all time
- painted the frescoes on the ceiling of the Sistine Chapel (one of his best known works)
- considered himself primarily a sculptor
    - his most famous sculptures include *David*, *Moses*, and *Pieta*
- had a really bad temper that even frightened his childhood friend, Pope Leo X (successor to Pope Julius II)
- was commissioned to paint the ceiling of the Sistine Chapel by Pope Julius II:
    - accepted the commission, but thought from the start that the plans of Julius II for the chapel ceiling were too simple
    - was allowed to change the plans as he wished, which was unheard of at that time

Machiavelli (1469-1527 A.D.):

- was an Italian historian, philosopher, humanist, and writer based in Florence during the Renaissance
- wrote *The Prince*, which promoted the ideas that:
    - the acquisition and expansion of political power are the means to restore and maintain order
    - political activity should not be limited by moral considerations
    - the prince acts on behalf of and for the sake of the state
    - princes must be willing to ignore their own consciences
        - they should do what is right if they can, but, if necessary, be prepared to do wrong

Piero della Francesca (1415-1498 A.D.):

- was the famous Umbrian artist who painted:
    - *Double Portrait of Battista Sforza*
    - *Frederico da Montefeltro*
    - *The Flagellation of Christ* (a controversial work)
- conceived the human figure as a volume in space
    - the outlines of his subjects have the grace, abstraction, and precision of geometric drawings
- is considered to be the best mathematician of his age

Simone Martini (1284-1344 A.D.):

- was a major figure in the development of early Italian painting and the International Gothic style
- served as court painter to King Robert
- was often considered Giotto's rival
- created the semi-great painting *The Siege of Montemassi*
- painted many frescoes and altarpiece panels, such as the *Virgin and Child* (painted for the Church of St. Catherine in Pisa)
- introduced the fresco technique into the Sienese school

Explorers and Scientists

Bartolomé de las Casas (1471-1566 A.D.):

- encouraged slave traders to bring slaves to the West Indies to "save" them from dying in the African mines
- was known as the "Apostle of the Indians"

Bartolomeu Dias (1451-1500 A.D.):

- was a Portuguese nobleman and explorer
- reached the southernmost tip of Africa in 1487
    o was the first European known to have done so
- named it the *Cape of Storms*
    o King John of Portugal renamed it *The Cape of Good Hope*, because of the great optimism engendered by the opening of a sea route to India and the East

Christopher Columbus (1451-1506 A.D.):

- sailed directly westward to find India and instead discovered the New World
- was patronized by Queen Isabella of Spain
- was a native of Genoa
- never received a fitting reward for his discovery (America is named after Amerigo Vespucci, the Florentine navigator who published the first account of the new lands)

Ferdinand Magellan (1480-1521 A.D.):

- Portuguese explorer who sailed from the Atlantic Ocean into the Pacific Ocean, and the first to cross the Pacific
- discovered the strait that now bears his name near the most southern point of Patagonia
- named the newly discovered ocean "Pacific" because it was so peaceful compared to the Atlantic
circumnavigated the globe in about 3 years

Francisco Pizarro (1471-1541 A.D.):

- tricked and imprisoned the Incan emperor, Atahualpa, then demanded a huge ransom for him
- collected the ransom, then killed Atahualpa anyway (1533 A.D.)
    - Atahualpa's death marked the end of the fabulous Andean dynasty

Hernando Cortes (1485-1547 A.D.):

- Spanish conquistador who organized an expedition from the Spanish settlements off the Gulf of Mexico
- brought large portions of mainland Mexico under the control of Spain
- invaded and conquered the Aztec empire
    - the Aztec leader, Montezuma, lost largely due to organizational collapse and lack of firearms

Henry VII (1457-1509 A.D.):

- outfitted a fleet for the exploration of the western seas
- put his fleet under the command of John Cabot and his son Sebastian (Venetian sailors doing business in England)
- benefited greatly from the successful voyages of the Cabots, who through their voyages gave England a title to the best portion of the North American coast

Nicolaus Copernicus (1473-1543 A.D.):

- published *On the Revolutions of the Heavenly Spheres* in 1543 A.D.
- believed in the heliocentric theory of the universe (where planets orbit the Sun and the Moon orbits the Earth)
- freely admitted that his idea of a spinning Earth in a sun centered universe was not original
    - it had first been proposed by Aristarchus some 2000 years earlier

Explorers and Scientists

Prince Henry the Navigator (1394-1460 A.D.)

- explored the coast of Africa, even reaching Morocco, in 1418 A.D.
- opened an observatory and a school for navigation to train his captains

Sir Francis Drake (1545-1595 A.D.):

- was a preeminent English sailor who sailed around the globe (1577-1579 A.D.)
    - he was knighted by Queen Elizabeth for that achievement
- helped the English Royal Navy destroy the Spanish Armada (in 1588 A.D.)
- fought the fleets of his sovereign's enemy, Philip II
- captured Spanish treasure vessels on the high seas
- pillaged warehouses and settlements on every Spanish shore in the Old and New World

Sir Walter Raleigh (1552-1618 A.D.):

- explored the central coasts of North America
- returned with such glowing accounts of the beauty and richness of the land visited, that, in honor of the Virgin Queen, it was named "Virginia"
- made the practice of smoking, which he had learned in the New World, popular

Vasco da Gama (died 1524 A.D.):

- was a Portuguese admiral and of the most successful explorers in the *Age of Discovery*
- commanded the first ships to sail directly from Europe to India
    - crossed the Indian sea and landed on the coast of Malabar in 1498 A.D.

Cultures

Accadians:

- were the original inhabitants of the Tigris-Euphrates river basin
- were thought to be of Turanian origin
- brought the art of hieroglyphic writing into the valley
- were renowned for the expansive clay tablet libraries in their capital city, Accad, which was known as the "City of Books"

Anglo-Saxons:

- were Germanic tribes—the ancestors of the English who settled in Great Britain
- resulted from the combination of the Angles (who became known as Anglos) and Saxons

Arabs:

- spurred on by a desire to master the learning of more established civilizations, which they understood would require the translation of documents into Arabic
- founded the House of Wisdom in 832 A.D. specifically for the translation and master of foreign sciences (this was set-up by the governing Caliph of Baghdad)
- based much of their knowledge on Arabic translations of earlier Greek texts
- directed research at specific fields that would yield useful information to their monarchs (e.g. mathematics, science, and especially medicine)
- emphasized the practical application of science and experimentation
- were particularly expert in astronomy, mathematics, medicine, and physics
- significantly contributed to the advancement of scientific knowledge during the period from 700-1100 A.D.
- peaked in its religious expansion around 900 A.D.

- o conquered all of Spain, which was the only major European country overthrown in its entirety by the Muslims
- o conquered only a small portion of France
- o was unable to penetrate Europe beyond that point
- broke into two major sects—the Shi'ites and the Sunni—after a disagreement as to who was the true successor of Muhammed
    - o the Sunni regard Abubekr as the successor
    - o the Shi'ites regard Ali, the fourth Caliph, as the true successor of the prophet

Assyrians:

- spoke the Semitic language
- organized a large, efficient army that was capable of fighting guerrilla warfare in various terrains
- developed the use of iron weapons and were the first to equip their army with them

Dorians:

- were a tribe of the Hellenes
- were a practical, unimaginative race
- focused on developing the body rather than the mind (e.g. gymnastics and the military)
- founded the city of Sparta (a rival to Athens)

Gauls:

- were a barbaric Celtic tribe
- invaded Macedonia in 279 B.C., and sacked Rome a century earlier
- inflicted terrible suffering on Macedonia and Greece
- settled in Asia Minor after being expelled from Europe, in a province they called Galatia
- were remembered in a famous Greek sculpture "The Dying Gaul" (which was often wrongly known as "The Dying Gladiator")

- terrified the Romans, due to ancient predictions in the Sibylline books stating that a portion of Roman territory would be occupied by the Gauls (the Roman Senate tried to fulfill this prophecy by burying two Gaul's alive in the public square)
- were angered by the extension of the Flaminian Way (a major road) which opened all of northern Italy to Rome, resulting in even heavier Roman colonization
- were finally defeated by the Romans, whose empire extended to the foothills of the Alps

Guebers:

- were fire worshippers who fled from Persia and took refuge in Gujarat (India) during that time
- came to be known as Parsees, where were members of the larger of the two Zoroastrian communities (the term Parsee wasn't used in Zoroastrian texts until the 17th century)

Goths:

- recrossed the Alps after pillaging Italy in 410 A.D.
- established camps in the south of Gaul and north of Spain, creating what became known as the Kingdom of the Visigoths

Hellenes:

- were inhabitants of Greece, though not the original ones
- are associated with classical Greek civilization (hellenistic)
- were preceded in Greece by the Mycenaeans
- ascribed the massive masonry of Pelasgian architecture to a race of giants called Cyclops
- were divided into four tribes: the Ionians, the Dorians, the Achaeans, and the Aeolians

Saracens (Arabians):

- was a term used by the Romans to describe people from the desert of Arabia, which eventually came to encompass all Arabs or worshippers of Islam
- worshipped idols before the arrival of Muhammad
- established Mecca as their holy city
- were a land of religious freedom during the days of the Roman Empire
- were responsible for much of the knowledge gained by two of the greatest scholars of the 13th century (Roger Bacon and Albertus Magnus)
- founded two schools in Spain which gave back the ancient Greek knowledge, plus much of the Arabian scientific knowledge, to Europe. One of those universities:
    - grew from medieval schools and cathedrals in Bologna, Italy in 1088 A.D.
    - was started by a group of students who employed scholars to teach them
    - primarily taught law, medicine, and theology

Spartans:

- residents of a Greek city-state that arose c. 650 B.C. and was independent for over 500 years
- were taught from early childhood that loyalty to the state was the prime reason for their existence
- stressed military training and obedience to authority
- abandoned infant boys who appeared too weak for military service
- sent boys to live in military barracks at age 7
- required military service of men from age 20 through age 60

Sumerians:

- emerged from the land of Sumer
- were located in Mesopotamia (which means "the land between the two rivers")
- were considered to be the world's first civilization
- were known for their technical achievements
- were eventually conquered by the Babylonians

Ottoman Turks (Ottoman Empire):

- were the most formidable Arab clans to accept the religion of Islam
- provided the military power that upheld and spread the creed of Muhammad
- established the powerful country of Turkey in Europe
- had their power checked by Tamerlane in the Battle of Angora, where he forced them to lift their siege on Constantinople
- laid siege to Constantinople again with 200,000 men led by their sultan, Mohammad II the Great (in 1453 A.D.)
- Took Constantinople by storm, which from the time of Constantine the Great had surmounted the dome of St. Sophia, was replaced by a crescent
- defeated the Serbs in the Battle of Kosovo
- lost their leader, Sultan Murad I, in that battle
- had conquered almost the entire Byzantine empire (which had served as a buffer between the Latin West and Muslim Middle East for centuries)
    - Constantinople stood alone' as a capital without a country, until it fell to the Turks in 1453 A.D. (after a siege of several months)

Cultures

Vandals:

- pushed into the north of Spain, occupying a large tract of country there (the area was later called Andalusia, in honor of its barbarian settlers)
- sacked Rome in 455 A.D., under the leadership of General Genseric
- raided Rome for a fortnight, taking every valuable thing they could from the capital, including the golden candlestick and 30,000 slaves

Vikings:

- sailed to Iceland in 860 A.D.
- first settled in Iceland 14 years later
- killed or drove out the Irish monks already on Iceland
- met each midsummer in an assembly called an Althing which acted as a legislative body, parliament, and court

Visigoths (Western Goths):

- were one of two main branches of the Goths (the Ostrogoths being the other)
- asked permission from the Roman emperor, Valens, to settle outside the Danube
- were soon followed there by Ostrogoths (Eastern Goths) who had been driven out of their homeland by the Huns
- joined the Ostrogoths in a successful war against Emperor Valens
- were later subdued and enlisted in the legions by anew Roman emperor, Theodosius

Languages

Aryan:

- the old Persian language

French:

- was influenced by the collision of old Latin speech (in Gaul) with that of the Teutonic invaders, which resulted in two distinct dialects:
    - Langue d'Oc, or Provencal, the tongue of the South of France and of the adjoining regions of Spain and Italy (still spoken in southern France)
    - Langue d'Oil, or French proper—the language of the North

Latin:

- was the language of ancient Rome
- is still taught by many universities
- used in biological classification
- exerted a great influence on Western Civilization
- was the language which many plays, poems, and speeches were written in

Semitic

- group of related languages spoken across the middle east, North Africa and the Horn of Africa
- common examples today are Arabic, Hebrew and Aramaic

Turanian

- arose in the area of Iran – exact location unknown
- later came to be associated with the Turks

Educated Romans:

- commonly spoke both Latin and Greek
- were taught rhetoric
- studied both Latin and Greek literature
- often traveled to Greece to study philosophy and rhetoric
- attended rhetorical schools (which became a central feature of Roman education after Greek scholars began traveling to Rome to teach)

Social and Cultural Facts

Primogeniture:

- was a concept introduced by the Normans (in 1066 A.D.) whereby the oldest son inherited his father's estate
- was the prevalent logic in Europe as the basis for the succession of kings
- was created to preserve the size of real estate (which was important to the aristocracy since their power and prestige was based on land ownership)

The Toga:

- was a distinctive garment of Ancient Rome (the white toga was the significant badge of Roman citizenship)
- consisted of a cloth about 20 feet (6 meters) long wrapped around the body over a tunic
- was worn by Roman men and boys (Roman boys exchanged their purple-hemmed togas for ones of white wool between the ages of 14 and 18)

The first English Census:

- was ordered in England in 1086 A.D. by William I
- was intended to evaluate the wealth of the land by providing a detailed survey of the entire country, including a record of:
    - all estates
    - all possessions great and small
    - the number of churches and monasteries, together with their level and sources of income
- resulted in the compilation of the Domesday Book (Domesday = Day of Judgement), which William could use to identify the most powerful men in the kingdom and the claims of each to the estates they held

Social and Cultural Facts

Spartan society slave labor:

- was provided by the Helots (conquered neighbors from Messenia and Laconia)
- freed the Spartans from agricultural production
- enabled them to focus on perfecting the craft of warfare

Slavery:

- began in the West Indies in response to the need for labor
  - the few Indians who lived on the islands, plus the indentured servants, were not enough to supply the labor demands on the growing plantations

Ostracism:

- was a Greek custom where a person could be banished from Athens for 10 years
- required 6000 votes against the person (in popular assembly) for a decree of banishment
- was generally exercised against politicians whose policies had failed
- resulted in the banished person's name being written on a piece of pottery or a shell

The women of Athens:

- lacked political rights
- could not attend, speak at, or vote in political assemblies
- could not hold political office
- could own property, including land (which was highly valued by the Greeks)
- generally received their share of their father's estate as a dowry

Slavery was:

- alive and well in Greece (slaves outnumbered their masters by as many as ten to one in Corinth, and four to one in Attica)
- regarded as a natural and legal relationship by the Greeks

The Egyptian preoccupation with death resulted in:

- the process of mummification
- the construction of pyramid tombs for the pharaohs

The Egyptian calendar:

- was 365 days long and highly accurate
- was developed in response to the Egyptian farmer's need to anticipate the annual flooding of the Nile
- suggested when farmers should plant and harvest their crops

The Egyptian religion:

- frequently centered around triad (group of three) gods which included a father, mother, and child
- Osiris (depicted by a bull), Isis (his wife and sister), and Horus (their son) are one such triad
- Osiris, Isis, and Horus were worshipped throughout Egypt, along with various animal gods

Egyptian believed that, at death:

- they would need to pass, by boat, through a dark and terrifying place called the Underworld (all Egyptian temples featured a sacred lake that depicted this crossing)
- preserving the body in death was important to keeping the soul alive
- in the "Underworld," the dead would answer to Osiris and 42 judges about their deeds in this life
- this "Judgment of the Dead" determined whether the body would be taken back to dishonor or allowed to pass into a happy afterlife

Social and Cultural Facts

Vocal Memnon:

- were low musical tones created when rays of the sun fell on the Colossi at Thebes
- believed by the Egyptians to be the statue greeting the mother sun
- likely produced by the sun's action upon the surface of the dew-covered rock
- only observed when the top of the statue lay on the ground as a result of an earthquake
- ceased when the statue was repaired

Four major Greek festivals:

- Olympian (the most famous, held every fourth year, with the interval between being called the Olympiad)
- Pythian
- Nemean
- Isthmian

Hellenism (Greek culture):

- was introduced to the Romans through their conquest of the Mediterranean
- eventually dominated the culture of Rome (according to Horace, the poet, "Captive Greece led her captor captive")

Medieval travel times:

- a trip from Venice to London took 4 weeks
- a trip from Venice to Lisbon took 7 weeks
- a trip from Venice to Damascus took 12 weeks

Innovations, Technology, and Achievements

The cuneiform system of writing:

- featured characters composed of wedge-like marks (as opposed to unbroken lines)
- is written using a triangular writing instrument that creates letters in the shape of wedge
- is named with the root word "cuneus" (meaning a wedge)

Alphabetical writing:

- was first introduced by the Phoenicians, who borrowed 22 hieratic characters from the Egyptians
- was passed by the Phoenicians to the Greeks, who
- then passed it on to the Romans, who
- then passed it on to the Germans

Early Greeks made many contributions to:

- modern geometry
- medicine
- mathematics
- astronomy
- philosophy

Romans intellectual achievements included:

- a codified legal system
- efficiencies in agriculture
- extensive road networks and shipping routes
- plumbing, hygiene, and sewage disposal improvements
- dams and aqueducts

Innovations, Technology, and Achievements

During the reign of Octavius (Augustus):

- Virgil composed his immortal epic of the *Aeneid*
- Horace wrote his famous odes
- Livy wrote his inimitable history
- Ovid wrote his *Metamorphoses*
- Christ was born in Bethlehem of Judea

Sumerian technical achievements included:

- the invention of the wheel
- charting the major constellations (astronomy)
- developing an advanced system of math (including a number system based on 60)
- using multiplication, division, and geometry in building projects and measuring fields
- developing large scale irrigation and drainage systems

Sumerian irrigation projects:

- were designed for flood control and managing the rivers
- were necessitated by the scarcity of rain, plus the unpredictable, catastrophic flooding of the Tigris and Euphrates rivers
- required organization, bureaucracy, and massive human effort to develop
- enabled farmers to grow more food than they could eat
- provided the material base for the emergence of civilization and cities
- opened the door for non-farmers to focus on other facets of civilization such as art, culture, and education

The Horse Collar:

- was an invention that enabled medieval farmers to use horses for plowing instead of cows
- was necessary for horse plowing since horses do not have shoulders like oxen
- greatly improved farming efficiency, since horses are faster, have greater endurance than oxen, and are able to follow voice commands

Innovations, Technology, and Achievements

Portuguese Navigators:

- incorporated technical innovations of German and Italian shipbuilders in the 14th and 15th centuries
- were instrumental in the maritime exploration and military conquests of Portuguese kings
- may have sailed around Australia's coast as early as 1542 A.D. (though they are not given credit for discovering it)
- explored the west coast of Africa, finding spices (which they could sell in Northern Europe) and gold
    - the re-export of West African spices from Lisbon to Flanders and Brabant became an important element of Portuguese trade

The Printing Press:

- was one of the most important technological innovations of Western civilization
- was invented during the Renaissance
- helped to rapidly spread the Protestant Reformation during the 1500s
- had an enormous impact on European society, bringing ideas, rhetoric, and how-to manuals to the people
- brought the Bible, in common languages, to the people, allowing them to read and interpret it for themselves
- was invented (from movable blocks or type) by Johannes Gutenberg of Mentz in 1438 A.D. (the first book off the press was a Latin Bible)
- is considered to be one of the most important advancements in the history of man

Diseases and Plagues

The disease of lycanthropy:

- is said to have affected Nebuchadnezzar II
- includes behavior where the victim:
    - imagines himself to be a beast
    - rejects normal food, clothing, and housing
    - fails to use articulate speech
    - may crawl on all fours (rather than walking)

The Black Death (Black Plague):

- was a contagious fever (plague) which entered Europe from the East and ravaged the continent from 1347-49 A.D.
- was called the Black Death because of the black spots which covered the bodies of sufferers
- killed more than a million Germans and as much as half of the English population
- resulted in economic stagnation and severe labor shortages
- was believed by many to be either caused by the devil or sent by God to punish man for his sins
- led many religious penitents, known as Flagellants, to resort to wander from town to town beating themselves with nail-ridden whips to win God's forgiveness (flagellantism was later condemned by the Catholic Church as heretical
- resulted in major changes in financial practices
    - labor shortages led to more favorable wages systems
    - the double-entry accounting system was developed
    - more sophisticated business and financial practices, such as the double-entry accounting system (which is the basis of modern accounting), credit finance, stock shares, and banking began to be developed

Business Facts

Tin:

- was a highly coveted metal used in the manufacture of bronze in Asia
- was fetched from Caucasus, on the eastern shore of the Euxine, by Phoenician sailors

Rome's Public Land System:

- was at the root of many social and economic troubles in Rome
- resulted in the greater part of land falling into the hands of the wealthy
- resulted into the people of Rome being divided into two new classes—instead of plebeians and patricians, there were now the rich and the poor, the possessors and the non-possessors, as someone famously said "a commonwealth of millionaires and beggars"

Guilds:

- were trade associations formed to advance the common interests of their members beginning around 1200 A.D.
- encouraged apprenticeships where apprentices worked for no pay except room and board, serving a master workman for 3-10 years (depending on the complexity of the trade to be learned)
- discouraged free enterprise
- maintained uniform quality and ethical standards by strictly regulating how a trade was practiced

Mercantilism:

- is an economic system which focuses on increasing a nation's wealth by government regulation of all the nation's commercial interests
- was adopted by many absolute monarchies as a way to promote prosperity and increase their revenue
- had national profit as its goal
- promoted colonialism through the idea that a nation should either produce everything needed for consumption, or import it from its own colonies
- emphasized state intervention in economic affairs, including subsidies for unprofitable industries and taxes on imports to destroy competition
- focused on the importance of a plentiful supply of gold and silver as a way to maintain a favorable balance of payments

The Industrial Revolution:

- was triggered by inventions and advances that built one upon the other
    - newly built canals allowed coal to be transported in bulk
    - Thomas Newcomen's mine pump led to
    - the invention of Watt's steam engine, which led to
    - modern factories and the Industrial Revolution

Crop Rotation:

- was a practice used by prior civilizations
- was "rediscovered" and begun by the Dutch, who previously left the land fallow every third year
- resulted in a boon in agricultural production

The Gold Florin:

- was first minted in Florence in 1252 A.D.
- became an important currency in European markets
- was the first European gold coin struck in sufficient quantities to play a significant commercial role since the 7th century
- were weighed on small portable scales by merchants and bankers to determine their worth
- made it difficult for anyone to cheat

In Medieval Commerce:

- luxury goods such as silk, jade and porcelain came overland all the way from China
- gold from Africa was carried by Islamic merchants across the Sahara Desert
- trading cities grew quickly since regular fairs were held by the merchants

People Groups (Entertainers)

Gladiators

- were armed combatants who entertained audiences in the Roman Empire through violent confrontations with other gladiators, wild animals, and condemned criminals
- were sometimes volunteers who were willing to risk their legal standing, social standing, and lives by appearing in the arena
- were most often despised as slaves, schooled under harsh conditions, socially marginalized, and segregated even in death
    - the last gladiator conflict in the Roman Amphitheater took place in 404 A.D. (the same year as the last military triumph of Rome, against Alaric)
    - this was not the first time the sport had been banned (Constantine had issued an imperial edict against it in 325 A.D.)
    - gladiating as a sport was finally brought to a halt by the brave martyr Telemachus, a Christian monk who ran into the amphitheater and rushed between the fighters, but was instantly killed by projectiles thrown by the audience (who were angered at the interruption of their sport)
    - the people soon repented of their act and Emperor Honorius himself was moved by the scene, thus, the death of Telemachus led to the final edict against gladiator fights as sport

Minnesingers:

- were the lyric poets or Troubadours of Germany
- were patronized by and flourished under the Hohenstaufen

People Groups (Entertainers)

Minstrels:

- entertained lords and ladies at medieval banquets and other events (the most important guests sat at a "high table" to distinguish them from the others)
- played a fiddle called a Rebec

Scalds (Bards):

- a professional poet, employed by a patron, such as a monarch or nobleman, to commemorate the patron's ancestors and to praise the patron's own activities

Troubadours:

- were the poets of southern France
- were the first voice of French literature
- were patronized by the Counts of Toulouse (who had also protected the Albigenses)
- were silenced by the same fierce persecution that decimated the Albigenses

Trouveurs:

- were the poets of Northern France
- composed in Langue d' Oil, or Old French tongue
- wrote epic, romantic poems about King Arthur, Alexander and Charlemagne and other heroic legends
- drew their material from the different races that blended to form France (Celtic, Graeco-Roman, and Teutonic)

People Groups (Political)

The Beggars:

- was a name assumed by the confederacy of Calvinist Dutch nobles and others who opposed Spanish rule in the Netherlands
- came about when a group of Dutch nobles requested that Duchess Margaret redress some grievances after the Inquisition.
    - when Margaret displayed great agitation, one of her councilors exclaimed, "Madam, are you afraid of a pack of Beggars?"
    - at a later banquet, a noble hung a beggar's wallet from his neck and proposed the toast, "Long live the Beggars."
    - the name, which was tumultuously adopted, became the party designation of the patriot Netherlanders during their long struggle with the Spaniards
    - The only reply of the Dutch government to the petition of the nobles was a decree termed the Moderation, which substituted hanging for burning in the case of condemned heretics. This resulted in image-breaking riots which destroyed many churches and art. The year following the outbreak of the Iconoclasts, Philip sent to the Netherlands a veteran Spanish army, headed by the Duke of Alva.

The Neo-Platonists:

- labored to restore Greek philosophy and worship (in a modified form)
- were in deep conflict with the teachers of Christianity
- lost the struggle between the two competing systems of thought

The Order of the Jesuits (the Society of Jesus):

- was founded by St. Ignatius Loyola, a native of Spain (1491-1556 A.D.)
- was a powerful agent in the counter-reformation to re-establish the Papal See
- did much to extend the authority and doctrines of the Roman Catholic Church around the world

The Sophists:

- were an infamous school of ancient Greek philosophers who charged money for education, engaged in shallow arguments, and preferred victory over truth
- were condemned and taunted by the better philosophers of their time, including Socrates
- were portrayed as deceptive, which led the modern meaning of the term "sophistry" today

People Groups (Religious)

Albigenses:

- were a group of Christians from south France whom Pope Innocent III viewed as heretics
- were attacked and massacred in a crusade called for by the Pope
    - in the same invasion, the property of their patron, the Count of Toulouse, was seized

Huguenots:

- rose into prominence in France despite the brutalities inflicted upon them
- were helped by Elizabeth of England and opposed by Philip II of Spain, who sent an army to attack them
- were brutally massacred in Paris on St. Bartholomew's Day (victim estimates range from 3,000 -10,000)
    - the massacre took place during the marriage of Princess Marguerite (sister to Charles IX) and Henry of Bourbon (Protestant king of Navarre), which had been proposed by Catherine de Medici to cement the treaty of St. Germain

Monastic orders:

- grew rapidly after the invention of mendicants (begging friars) by St. Dominic and St. Francis
- could possess any amount of wealth, though the monks remained poor individually

Puritans:

- were so named due to their desire for a purer form of worship than the Anglican
- felt the Church of England (which had been established by Elizabeth) was only half-reformed
- were less zealous than the Separatists, who hated anything that bore resemblance to Roman worship

People Groups (Social Classes)

The Hetairae:

- were a class of Greek women noted for their brilliancy of mind
- were promoted to Greek men as a source of social and intellectual sympathy and friendship outside the family circle
- included as one of their most noted members Aspasia (friend of Pericles)
- generally had a harmful influence on Greek social morality
- were allowed to watch both Greek comedies and tragedies (other Greek women were not allowed to watch comedies, which were considered too degrading for them)

Patricians:

- one of the two major social classes in Roman society
- members of the 3 original Roman tribes
- the only Romans to have political rights, at the first

Plebians:

- were one of the two major social classes in Roman society
- comprised mostly of citizens of conquered cities and refugees who sought asylum in Rome
- devoid of political rights
- allowed to acquire property and enjoy personal freedom

Painting and Sculpture

Famous Renaissance Artists included:

- Leonardo da Vinci, Michelangelo, Raphael, and Titian (Italian)
- Jan van Eyck, Roger van der Weyden, Peter Bruegel (Flemish)
- Albrecht Durer (German)

Literary Facts and Forms

Socratic Dialogue:

- is a type of Greek prose preserved in the works of Plato (Socrates most famous student) and Xenophon
- involved the discussion of moral and philosophical problems
- often featured Socrates as the main character
- when written by Plato, deeply reflected his own genius (though he attributed them to Socrates)

Pantomime:

- became popular in Roman theatre because it was impossible for actors to make their voices heard throughout structures so large
- the many different nationalities of a Roman gathering made it so that signs where the only language that could be readily understood by all

Satire:

- was common in Rome
- rose from the degradation during the reigns of Caligula, Nero and Domitian
- was mastered by Lucilius (148 B.C.), Persius, and Juvenal

Ancient Persian literature:

- was mostly religious
- included a sacred book called the Zend-Avesta (the oldest part of that book, called the Vendidad, included laws, incantations, and mythical tales)

Edda

- ancient Icelandic literature
- contained in two 13th century books
- prose part referred to as the Younger Edda
- poetry part referred to as Elder Edda
- contained detailed information on Germanic mythology

Greek drama:

- began with the recital of a single speaker
- progressed to dialogue between two speakers (a concept which was introduced by Thespis around 536 B.C., resulting in the term "Thespian" being applied to tragic drama)
- eventually featured three speakers (the classical number)

Literary Works

Utopia:

- was a book written by Sir Thomas More in 1516 A.D. which, like Plato's *Republic*, described a place that was perfect in its social, political, and moral aspects
- was set in an imaginary island located somewhere off the coast of the New World
- reflected More's concerns for the economic, political, and social problems of his day
- promoted the concept of equal social status for all
- included many communist and socialist elements
- replaced private property with communal ownership
- limited work to 9 hours per day
- provided for everyone according to their needs, regardless of their occupation

Iliad:

- is a Homeric epic poem
- tells the story of the Trojan War and "wrath of Achilles"

Odyssey:

- is a second Homeric epic poem (and sequel to Iliad)
- narrates the story of the long wanderings of Odysseus (Ulysses) up and down many seas while seeking his native Ithaca
- took place after the fall of Ilios
- may portray the punishment of the gods on Odysseus (Ulysses) for not respecting the horse of Athena
- also told the story of Penelope, the wife of Odysseus (Ulysses), who despite being sought by many suitors during the absence of her husband, remained faithful

Works and Days:

- a didactic, epic poem by Hesiod that tells of common men and everyday duties
- sort of a farmer's calendar, in which industry is praised and lucky/unlucky days for doing certain types of work are listed
- written in practical lines
- includes maxims on morality and beautiful descriptive passages about the changing seasons

The Song of the Nibelungen:

- was one of the first national pieces of literature produced in Germany
- was a great German medieval epic
- featured Siegfried as its hero (the Achilles of Teutonic legend and song)
- were patronized by the Hohenstaufen

The Republic:

- was a Socratic Dialogue written by Plato
- concerned the definition of justice and the character of the ideal city-state

The *Secret Inner Struggle or the Secreta Secretorumis:*

- was written by Petrach, poet laureate of Rome and great pre-Renaissance humanist
- recorded three secret dialogues between Petrarch and St. Augustine in the presence of Truth, where Augustine admonished future thinkers to "Reflect upon yourself"
- was an autobiographical treatise and counterpart to *St. Augustine's Confessions*, which were written in the 4th century A.D.

"The Garden of Earthly Delights" was:

- one of the most famous paintings from the Renaissance era
- painted by Hieronymus Bosch

El Cid:

- was the start of Castilian or Spanish literature in the 12th century
- was a grand national romance poem that grew out of the feelings inspired by the struggle between Spanish Christians and Mohammedan Moors
- is also known by the titles El Cantar de mio Cid, The Lay of the Cid, The Song of the Cid, El Poema del Cid—although the original title is unknown

Religions

Shamanism:

- has been shown by archaeologists to be the religion of the Accadians
- involved a belief in good and evil spirits
- evoked charms and magic rites to avert the influence of the evil spirits, who were considered to be the most powerful type

Roman Catholicism:

- dominated much of Europe during the 1500's
    - Lutheranism was prominent in Germany
    - the Eastern Orthodox Religion held sway in Russia
    - Islam continued to be dominant in the Arab world

The Chaldaean religion:

- included a story of origins that was remarkably like the first chapters of Genesis
- tell of the creation of the world, an ancestral paradise, a Tree of Life with angel guardians, the Great Deluge, and the Tower of Babel
- includes the 12-part epic of Izdubar (Herakles of Greece), which recount the 12 labors of the sun in its yearly passage through the 12 signs of the zodiac

Gods

Marduk:

- the highest Babylonian god
- connected with magic, judgment, water, and vegetation

Apollo:

- the Greek god of prophecy
- known as the "revealer"

Dionysus:

- the Greek god of wine
- the motivation for the songs and dances behind Greek drama (both tragedy and comedy)
- is known as Bacchus (a Roman god)

Heracles (Hercules):

- a Greek sun god
- likely originated from Izdubar, a Chaldaean sun god (the fables told about both were the same)

Mars was:

- the Roman god of war and fabled father of the Roman race, who considered themselves to be the "children of Mars"
- second only in importance to Jupiter
- the root of the name for the month of March, which was the first month of the Roman year, when games and festivals were celebrated in honor of Mars

Yahweh

- the name of God in the Bible commonly vocalized as Jehovah
- God delivered Israel from the Egyptians and gave them the 10 Commandments

Mythological Beliefs

Major characters in the siege of Troy:

- Helen, the beautiful wife of Menelaus, king of Sparta
- Paris, son of Priam
- Agamemnon, brother of Menelaus and "king of men"
- Achilles, the "lion-hearted" central character of the Trojan War and greatest Greek warrior of Homer's *Iliad*
- Ulysses, who was known for being crafty
- Ajax, "the swift son of Oileus"
- the aged Nestor

Major events in the siege of Troy:

- Paris captured Helen and held her hostage
- Agamemnon sailed across the Aegean in an attempt to rescue Helen from the Trojan shores
- the Greeks and their allies held the city of Troy in siege for ten years
- Troy was finally seized by use of the deceptive Trojan Horse
- archaeological evidence shows that a city like Troy did exist, although it may not have held that name
- the ruins of Troy and Mycenae and the Greek Bronze Age were discovered in 1873 by German archaeologist Heinrich Schliemann, who believed that Homer's accounts were not fiction, but historical fact

Argonautica (Jason and the Argonauts):

- is the tale of men who sailed on the Argo (their fifty-oar galley) in a successful quest for the fabled "golden fleece"
- the only surviving Hellenistic epic
- included Heracles, Theseus, and Orpheus (the musician)
- may symbolize the successful maritime expeditions of the Pelasgians

Gorgon (in Greek mythology):

- any of three sisters whose hair was woven with venomous snakes
- a scene so terrifying that gazing upon it chilled the beholder to stone

Hades:

- the vast realm of departed souls
- a region beneath the earth in the ancient Greek cosmos, reached by subterranean passages

Tartarus:

- a deep, gloomy place, a pit, or an abyss used as a dungeon of torment and suffering that resides beneath Hades or the underworld in Greek mythology
- secured by strong gates of brass
- related to the words Tartar and Tartarian (hellish)

Elysian Fields:

- a western section of the underworld in Greek mythology
- the home of the souls of heroes and poets
- supposedly ruled by Kronos

Philosophical and Religious Concepts and Beliefs

Scholasticism:

- was a form of philosophy that grew within the schools established by Charlemagne
- began in the theological world of the 11th and 12th centuries, particularly with the work of Peter Abelard
- was a fusion of Christianity and Aristotelian logic
- tried to reconcile classical philosophy (especially of Aristotle) with the early Christian patristic writers
- sought to apply reason and logical analysis to church doctrines and the study of theology, using logical arguments instead of the spiritual intuition which was relied on in the earlier (patristic) period
- was expounded by teachers known as "Schoolmen" (including Albertus Magnus, Roger Bacon, Thomas Aquinas, and Duns Scotus
- was especially championed by the Schoolman Thomas Aquinas, who was called the "Angel of the Schools" (Aquinas died in 1274 A.D.)
- peaked in the 13th century
- Taught the seven liberal arts, which consisted of:
    - Trivium (the course of Grammar, Logic, and Rhetoric), and
    - Quadrivium (Arithmetic, Geometry, Astronomy, and Music)

Humanism:

- flourished during the Renaissance:
- were more interested in the human than the divine
- extended their studies well beyond the theology that dominated medieval scholarship, studying arts, language, social problems, ethics, and philosophy (subjects still referred to as the "humanities") rather than subjects like economics

Philosophical and Religious Concepts and Beliefs

Stoicism:

- believed that emotions such as fear, envy, or passionate love arose from false judgments
- strove to achieve moral and intellectual perfection
- promoted a stern notion of morality which involved life in accordance with nature and controlled by virtue
- taught perfect indifference to everything external (hence the meaning of the word "stoic" today)

The Divine Right of Kings:

- was a doctrine that came to England with Mary Queen of Scot's successor, James I
- promoted the idea that kings received their authority from God, making it absolute and unquestionable
- implied that any attempt to depose a king or restrict his power ran contrary to the will of God and constituted heresy
- bolstered the arguments of theorists of that era (the 1600's) that government was divinely ordained in order to enable man to live in an organized society

The Five Pillars of Islam:

- belief in Allah as the one true God and Muhammad as his prophet (shahada)
- daily prayers – performed five times facing toward mecca (salat)
- almsgiving (zakat)
- fasting during the month of Ramadan (sawm)
- pilgrimage to city of Mecca at least once during a person's lifetime (hajj)

Ramadan:

- is the Islamic month of fasting, in which participating Muslims refrain from eating, drinking, smoking and sex during daylight hours
- is intended to teach Muslims about patience, spirituality, humility and submission to God

- takes place during the 9th month of the Islamic calendar (the month in which, according to Muslim tradition, the Koran was given to Muhammad)

Apostolic Succession:

- is the Catholic teaching that bishops represent a direct, uninterrupted line of continuity from the apostles of Jesus Christ
  - Catholics teach that the Bishop of Rome is in a direct line of succession, going back to the apostle Peter, who they teach is the first Bishop of Rome

The Augsburg Confession (Augustana) was:

- the formula of belief of the adherents of Luther
- drawn up by Luther's successor Melanchthon, and laid before the Imperial Diet assembled at Augsburg by Charles V in 1530

The Doctrine of Petrine Supremacy:

- is the belief that bishops of Rome hold a preeminent position in the church over all other bishops and patriarchs
- argues that the Roman church was founded by St. Peter himself, into whose hands Christ had given the keys of the kingdom of heaven, making him the chief apostle and the first bishop of Rome
- engendered belief in the papacy as head of the western Christian church

Social and Religious Movements

The Protestant Reformation:

- had its beginnings with the Lutherans and Calvinists, long before Henry VIII broke off from the Catholic church
- was furthered by King Henry VIII's decision to break England off from the Catholic Church in Rome and declare himself head of the church
- split the community of Christians into two camps: Catholics and Protestants
- pitted two incompatible theologies against each other
- contributed to the start of a number of religious wars in Europe:
    - The Thirty Years' War
    - The War of Spanish Succession
    - English, French, German, and Dutch civil wars
        - the French and German civil wars each dragged on for 30 years
        - the Dutch civil war lasted for 80 years

The Italian Renaissance:

- was a cultural movement that sprang up around the beginning of the 14th century and continued until the 17th century
- fostered a great enthusiasm for Greek and Latin literature and art
- was also known as the New Birth

The Inquisition:

- was established by the Catholic church for the purpose of detecting and punishing heresy
- established a tribunal, known as the "Holy Office," which became an instrument of the most incredible cruelty—burning thousands at the stake and condemning many others to endure penalties that were scarcely less terrible
- was directed against enemies of the papacy, including Moors, Jews, and any among the nobility or clergy who dared to oppose

Religious and Philosophic Texts

The Old Testament (Hebrew religious text):

- presents Moses as the great lawgiver
- presents the Ten Commandments as:
  - the Law given by God directly to Moses on Mount Sinai for the people of Israel
  - the basis of the covenant agreement
  - the definition of how God expects his people to live

The Talmud:

- is a collection of Hebrew customs and traditions that includes comments from the rabbis
- is the central text of mainstream Judaism
- contains the writings of Philo (Jewish philosopher who lived in Alexandria just before the birth of Christ)
- includes the antiquities of the Jews and the Jewish Wars by the historian Josephus (historian who lived during the 1st century after Christ)

Greek Oracles:

- were believed to be:
  - special communications from the gods delivered through individuals
  - made by Zeus and Apollo
- included, as their most renowned:
  - those believed to have been delivered by Zeus at Dodona, in Epiris
  - those of Apollo at Delphi in Phocis

The Qur'an (Koran in non-Islamic cultures):

- contains the doctrines of Muhammadanism, or Islam (which means submission)
- is the sacred book of the Muslims, who believe that God has revealed Himself through four holy men:
    - Moses (through the Pentateuch)
    - David (through the Psalms)
    - Jesus (through the Gospels)
    - Muhammad (the Koran)
- is the bible of Islam, regarded by Muslims as the true word of Allah (God)
- was, according to Muslim tradition, revealed to Muhammad in segments by the angel Gabriel over a span of 20 years
- is believed to have been written down by Muhammad's companions during his lifetime
- was standardized and produced in large numbers for distribution to the Islamic empire in 653 A.D.

Battles and Wars

The Battle of Marathon:

- was fought between the Athenians (Greeks) and the Persians, and won by the Greeks
- a legend claims that a message was delivered by the fleet runner Pheidippides, who declared "Victory is ours" and fell dead
- The fleet runner had run approximately 26 miles to deliver his message

The Dorian Invasion:

- is a concept devised by historians of Ancient Greece to explain the replacement of pre-classical dialects and traditions the ones that prevailed in Classical Greece
- involves a Greek legend asserting that the Dorians took possession of the Peloponnesus in an event called the Return of the Heracleidae
- allegedly happened 80 years after the Trojan War, and 100 years after the exile appointed by the Fates

The Second Messenian War:

- took place sometime between 750 and 650 B.C.
- involved Messenia, a district of Peloponnesus which, together with Laconia, had been invaded by the Dorians
- was fought by the Spartans, who were inspired by the poetry of Tyrtaeus (an Attic poet)

Battles and Wars

The First Sacred War:

- was fought in 600-590 B.C.
- was a 10-year crusade by the Amphictyons against the cities for Crissa and Cirrha
- was sparked by the robbery of the Delphian temple treasures by the two cities
- resulted in:
    - cities of Crissa and Cirra were conquered and leveled
    - wrath of the gods invoked on any who dared to rebuild them
    - spoils of war were devoted to providing musical contests to honor the Delphian Apollo.

The Persian Wars:

- involved two invasions of Greece by the Persians
- took place between 490 and 479 B.C.
- involved the battles of Thermopylae (Hot Gateway), Plataea, Artemisium and Salamis
- resulted in the defeat of the Persians, the survival of Greek culture, and the destruction of the myth of Persian invincibility

The Battle of Thermopylae (or "Hot Gates"):

- preceded the burning of Athens by Xerxes (the Persian king)
- was named for several hot springs at the foot of the cliffs near a narrow pass between the mountain and the sea
- took place in the Valley of Thermopylae:
    - was a critical pass for invaders traveling from northern to southern Greece
    - was the site for a famous battle where 300 Spartans fought to the death against an invading, much larger, Persian force

The Peloponnesian War:

- was fought between Athens and Sparta
- happened towards the end of the life of Pericles (431-404 B.C.)
- resulted from rivalry between the two cities
- has traditionally been divided into three phases

The Battle of Leuctra:

- involved 6000 Theban soldiers who overthrew a Spartan force twice their size
- was the first time the Spartans were ever fairly defeated in open battle
- broke the military grip of the Spartans
- marked the rise of the Thebans as a new power in the Hellenic world
- took place in 371 B.C.

The First Punic War (264-241 B.C.):

- was the first of three wars fought between Carthage and the Romans—the two strongest powers of the Mediterranean
- began over the possession of the island of Sicily and continued for a hundred years
- was similar to the war between Athens and Sparta, but on a larger scale
- was won by Rome
- was the first step in the creation of the Roman Empire (the second step came after the Second Punic War, when Rome acquired most of the Western Mediterranean, while the final step was the possession of Sardinia and Corsica)

The First Servile War (135-132 B.C.):

- was an unsuccessful rebellion of slaves against their masters in the Roman Republic
- involved 200,000 slaves, who fought for 3 years before being crushed by Rome

Battles and Wars

The Battle of Pharsalus (48 B.C.):

- was Caesar's decisive victory
- resulting in Pompey fleeing to Egypt, where he was assassinated

The Germanic Invasions:

- were perpetrated by two northern tribes, the Teutones and Cimbri
- took place while Rome was destabilized due to internal struggles between social classes, and also a war with Africa
- resulted in the defeat of the northern tribes by Marius
- was quickly followed by a divisive internal revolt in Rome by the Marsians (over the issue of citizenship)

The Crusades (Holy Wars):

- agitated all of Europe during the 12th and 13th centuries
- were military expeditions by the Christian nations of Europe to rescue the holy places of Palestine from the Mohammedans (the Saracen caliphs had been replaced by the Seljukian Turks, a prominent Tartar tribe who, unlike their predecessors, persecuted and insulted Christian pilgrims to the Holy City)
- did much to weaken the power of the nobles, who frequently sold or mortgaged their estates to raise money for their expeditions
- resulted in power and influence passing from the nobles into the hands of kings or wealthy urban merchants

The Second Crusade:

- started in 1146 when Edessa was plundered by Turks
- accomplished nothing for the Christian world.
- several orders of knights arose whose object, above all the orders, was to care for the sick and wounded crusaders, entertain Christian pilgrims, guard the holy places, and battle for the cross (Hospitallers, Teutonic Knights, Knights Templar)

The Third Crusade (1189-1192 A.D.):

- was caused by the capture of Jerusalem by Saladin, the sultan of Egypt
- featured Richard the Lionhearted (Richard I) as the hero of the Christian knights

The Children's Crusade (1212 A.D.):

- resulted in the deaths of hundreds of thousands of children 12 years old and under
- started when the children set off to save the Holy <u>Sepulchre</u>
- many who didn't die were sold as slaves in Alexandria

The crusades:

- spurred the development of numerous city republics, especially in Italy (a similar outcome resulted from the military campaigns of ancient Greece)

The Hundred Years War:

- began when Edward III laid claim to the French crown after the death of Charles IV
- 1336-1453 A.D.
- resulted from Edward's claim to the throne through his mother, Isabella of France
- was precipitated by England's war with Scotland (France angered England by aiding and encouraging Scotch rebels)

The Battle of Crecy (1346 A.D.)

- dealt a death blow to feudalism, chivalry, and warfare by mail-clad knights with battles and axes
- brought in a new age of battle by common foot soldiers with bow and gun

The Third Battle of Lepanto (1571 A.D.):

- was a struggle involving more than 600 ships and 200,000 men on the western coast of Greece between the Christian fleet of Philip and the Ottoman Turks
- resulted in the destruction of almost the entire Ottoman fleet
- gave the Holy League temporary control over the Mediterranean
- protected Rome from invasion
- prevented the Ottomans from advancing into Europe

The "Eighty Years War":

- began in 1568 A.D. when the Netherlands declared independence and revolted against the Spanish Empire
- ended in 1648 when Spain formally acknowledged the independence of the Dutch

The Spanish Fury (1576 A.D.):

- was a revolt of Spanish soldiers upset about not being paid
- led to an alliance between Holland, Zealand, and the other 15 provinces of the Netherlands which is known as the Pacification of Ghent

Other Disputes

The "Investiture Controversy":

- began as a dispute in 1075 A.D. between Pope Gregory VII and Germany's King <u>Henry IV</u> over the appointment of competing candidates to be Bishop of Milan
    - Gregory:
        - claimed to be God's vicar on Earth and as such, to have supreme power over all Christendom, including the right to depose kings and emperors
        - intended to free the Church from royal interference in the election of Church officials
        - decreed, in 1075 A.D., that no one could receive investiture of a church, abbey, or bishop from the hand of a king, emperor or any other lay person (e.g. it had to be from the pope)

The "Iconoclastic Controversy":

- is the dispute about the worship of images in church history
- broke out in the 8th century between the Greek churches of the East and the Latin churches of the West
    - Leo the Isaurian, who attained the throne of Constantinople in 717 A.D., was a zealous Iconoclast (image-breaker) who was excommunicated, leading to a permanent split in the church.

Other Disputes

The Great Schism:

- was a division that resulted from a dispute over the papal election in 1377 A.D.
- resulted when two churchmen both claimed the title of pope
- led to much criticism (and a reduction of power) of the Catholic church
- caused great numbers of clerics to conclude that only a general council of the church could end the schism and bring about reform
    - was brought to an end in 1417 A.D. as a result of the Council of Constance, which was first called for in 1414 A.D. by Sigismund, the Holy Roman Emperor at that time

The "Struggle of the Orders"

- was the social conflict between the patricians and the plebeians in the 5th century B.C.
- resulted from the lack of plebeian rights (to hold office, intermarry with patricians, have political representation)
- ceased when the plebeians forced the patricians to concede by refusing to serve in the Roman army until their demands were met
- changed Roman life by bringing about
    - "The Twelve Tables" (which gave plebeians full protection under the law)
    - "The Tribune" (which allowed plebeians to elect their own officials), and the
    - "Lex Canuleia Law" (which legalized intermarriage between patricians and plebeians)

Military Facts

Phalanx:

- was a rectangular military formation used in ancient Greek warfare
- was originated by Philip of Macedon
- was as renowned in the military history of Macedonia as the "legion" is in Rome

The Spanish Armada:

- was sent to invade England by King Philip II of Spain
- was defeated by the British Royal Navy in 1588 A.D. (an event which marked the beginning of the decline of the Spanish empire)
- was repelled by heavy English guns mounted on ships, which proved to be a decisive advantage not only in this victory, but in establishing England as the world's dominant naval power (weather was also a factor in the defeat of the Spanish Armada)

The "gangway" or "boarding plank" on ships:

- was invented by the Romans to make up for their deficiencies in naval warfare
- was allowed to fall upon an approaching galley, whereupon Roman soldiers would rush onto the other ship and engage in hand-to-hand conflict (in which they were unequaled)
- was used against the superior navy of the city of Carthage

Greek Fire:

- was a bituminous compound used by the Greeks to thwart an Arab attack on Constantinople

The fall of the Roman Empire:

- came about in 476 A.D. (5th century) after repetitive raids by barbarian tribes
- brought an end to the empire after an existence of 1229 years
- brought the collapse of government and institutions
    - it was churches and monasteries that kept social welfare and education alive in Europe
    - churchmen assumed many of the duties that government normally would have fulfilled
- has been attributed:
    - to the free distribution of grain, a practice begun by Gaius Gracchus (which led to idleness and vice)
    - the rise of Christianity (by Edward Gibbon in 1776)
        - Gibbon argued that Christianity, by promoting belief in a better life after death, fostered indifference to the present, thereby sapping Roman desire to make personal sacrifices for the good of the nation

Treaties and Leagues

The Religious Peace of Augsberg:

- was established in 1555
- stated that every prince should be able to choose between the Catholic and Lutheran religions

The Magna Carta:

- a great charter of English liberty
- put the unwritten rights and obligations of feudal customs between a king and his vassals on paper
- promoted the idea that a monarch's power was limited rather than absolute
- stated that no freeman should be deprived of life, liberty, or property "save by the legal judgment of his peers"
- required that no taxes (except for specified feudal aids) should be imposed "save by the Common Council of the realm"
- resulted after King John failed to retake Normandy from the French in 1215 A.D.
    - King John's barons rebelled and forced him to sign the Magna Carta

The Treaty (or Peace) of St. Germain (1570 A.D.):

- ended the third of the French Wars of Religion
- provided that Protestants would be allowed to hold public offices in France
- promised the marriage of Princess Marguerite to Henry of Bourbon (a Protestant)
- created short-lived peace, due to the massacre of Huguenots on St. Bartholomew's Day in Paris

Treaties and Leagues

The Edict of Nantes (1598 A.D.):

- was published by Henry of Bourbon
- granted the Huguenots freedom of worship, opened to them all offices and employments, and gave them a large number of fortified towns, including the important city of La Rochelle

The Treaty of Westphalia:

- was signed in 1648
- gave equal opportunities to Catholics, Lutherans, and Calvinists
- marked the end of the Reformation Era and the beginning of the Political Revolution

The Hanseatic League:

- was a trading group formed by German trading cities that banded together during the 13th century
- featured Bruges, London, Bergen, and Novgorod as the four most noted centers of trade in the confederation
- struggled with a severe economic decline in the 14th century after the plague killed more than a third of the population of Europe

The Peace of Pericles (Thirty Year Truce):

- ended the war between Sparta and Athens in 445 B.C.
- required Athens to surrender any ambitions for a land empire and be content with naval supremacy
- required Athens to share leadership of the Hellenic cities with Sparta

The Peloponnesian League:

- was led by the Greek city of Sparta
- included most of the major land powers of Peloponnesus and central Greece, together with Corinth (a sea power)
- provided protection and security to its members (specifically, Sparta)
- assisted the Greeks in their resistance to Persian invasions
- fought against Athens during the Peloponnesian War

The Latin League:

- was a confederation of about 30 villages and tribes in the region of Latium near ancient Rome, organized for mutual defense
- was broken up after 3 years of hard fighting, when the plebeians joined the patricians to fight against it

The Confederacy of Delos:

- was formed shortly after the battle of Plataea to enable the confederates to fight more effectively against the Persians
- had Aristides as its first president (477 B.C.)
- set the sacred island of Delos as the repository of its common funds
- included the Ionian states, the islands of the Aegea, and some of the states of Greece

Quotes and Anecdotes

"He made me the herdsman of this land, for he discerned that I would keep it in order for him; he entrusted to me that which he protected."
One of the pharaohs of Egypt

The prophet Ezekiel described the length and cruelty of the Sargon II's siege of Samaria: "Every head was made bald, and every shoulder was peeled."
Ezekiel 29:18

"The master of the monstrous... the discoverer of the unconscious."
Carl Jung, speaking about the great painter Hieronymus Bosch

In a Roman legend the female prophet Sibyl offered to sell the Roman king Tarquin 9 books containing prophecies regarding the Roman people at a very steep price. He refused, so she burned three of the books and offered the remaining 6 at the same price. Again he refused, and again she burned three books and offered the remaining 3 at the original price. Fearing the books would forever be lost should he refuse, he agreed to buy the remaining 3 books (which were later kept safe in a temple) at the original asking price.

Seleucus Nicator, ruler of Seleucid, was said to be "the greatest founder of cities that ever lived."

Tyre – A City in Lebanon, was known as "bare as the top of a rock"

The Stone of Scone had this inscription: "Should fate not fail, where'er this stone be found, The Scot shall monarch of that realm be crowned"

Richard the Lionheart reportedly said he would "sell the city of London if he could find a purchaser"

Carlyle said of gunpowder "It made all men of the same height"

The quote said when a lord knighted a knight was "In the name of God, of St. Michael, and of St. George, I dub thee knight: be brave, bold, and loyal."

The Queen of Sheba said after viewing Solomon's wisdom and wealth: "The half was not told me".

Cardinal Richelieu said "I shall trample all opposition under foot, and then cover all errors with my scarlet robe"

Aeschylus through his dramas promoted the idea that promoted the idea, through his dramas, that "no mortal may dare raise his heart too high" and that "Zeus tames excessive lifting up of heart"

King Porus, when asked how he should be treated, answered "like a king"

Draco's laws were so cruel, it was said that "they were written, not in ink, but in blood"

Polyxena was said to have carried "in her eyelids the whole history of the Trojan War"

Euclid, when asked by King Ptolemy for an easier way to learn geometry, answered "there is no royal road to geometry".

Herodotus called Egypt a "gift of the Nile"

Pindar is known for the phrase "become that which thou art"

Pythagoras viewed the solar system as being a "harmony of the spheres"

Socrates talked about death the night before he was poisoned in what became known as the "Socratic Dialogue"

Draco's laws would punish small crimes with great severity, therefore, "Draconian" came to refer to actions that are unusually harsh

Solon was known for saying to "count no man happy until he is dead."

Caesar, before he was killed, exclaimed "Et tu, Brute," which means "Even you, Brutus?" when Brutus raised his dagger

Caligula stated at one time that he wished "the people of Rome had but one neck"

Constantine was converted when, during a military campaign, he reputedly saw a luminous cross in the sky with the inscription "with this sign you will conquer"

Attila the Hun was a warrior so fierce that the grass never grew again "where once the hoof of Attila's horse had trod"

Hannibal was once called the "the foremost man of his race and his time, perhaps the mightiest military genius of any race and of any time."

Caliph Omar burned the entire library of Alexandria, saying "If these books agree with the Koran, they are useless; if they disagree, they are pernicious: in either case they ought to be destroyed."

Horace the poet said that "captive Greece led her captor captive"

Someone famously said that Rome was "a commonwealth of millionaires and beggars".

When Margaret, Duchess of Parma, displayed great agitation because of the protests of the Dutch nobles against Philips rules, one of her councilors exclaimed, "Madam, are you afraid of a pack of Beggars?" At a later banquet, a noble hung a beggar's wallet from his neck and proposed the toast, "Long live the Beggars."

The Iliad tells the story tells the story of the Trojan War and "wrath of Achilles"

Augustine admonished future thinkers to "Reflect upon yourself"

Romans considered themselves to be "children of Mars"

The fleet runner, Pheidippides, ran 26 miles back to Athens and gave word of the Battle of Marathon to the citizens declaring "Victory is ours" and fell dead

The Magna Carter stated that no freeman should be deprived of life, liberty, or property "save by the legal judgment of his peers"

The Magna Carter required that no taxes (except for specified feudal aids) should be imposed "save by the Common Council of the realm"

Famous Nicknames

Margaret of Denmark—"the Semiramis of the North"

Bartolome Las Casas—"the Apostle of the Indians"

Pontifus Maximus—"the pope"

Roman Senate—"council of old men"

Absolute ruler of Rome—"dictator"

Roman informer or spy—"delator"

Castle of Hapsburg in Switzerland was called the "cradle of the family"

Netherlands – bears "United Provinces of the Netherlands" as its official name

Wood from Phoenicia – called "The Cedars of Lebanon"

Seleucid – "the greatest founder of cities that ever lived"

Constantinople – Known as the "City of Constantine"

The Parthenon was known as the "residence of the virgin goddess Athena"

The House of Vesta was known as "House of the Vestal Virgins"

The leader of the College of Pontiffs was called "Pontifex Maximus" or the "Chief Bridge-builder"

The House of Austria was called the "cradle of the family"

Pharoahs derived their name from a word that means "high house"

The Roman Senate was composed of the "fathers" and called the "Council of Old Men"

delators – people who acted as spies

A Greek "polis" included an "association of kinsmen" that made up the city itself

Chivalry was also referred to as "The Flower of Feudalism"

The title "Prince of Wales" was assigned to Welsh chiefs who ruled over an independent Wales

The "Patriarchal Age" of Hebrew History covered the lifespan of the three Hebrew patriarchs: Abraham, Isaac, and Jacob

The "Middle Ages" was the period of history between the Classical Period and the Renaissance, from approximately the 5th to 15th century A.D.

The "Dark Age of the Papacy" was a 70-year period also known as the Babylonian captivity

Sargon of Akad was called the "Chaldean Solomon" by the scholar Sayce

Geoffrey Chaucer was called the "Father of English Poetry"

The dilemma the rich faced when Henry VII demanded all their money was known as "Morton's Fork"

Henry VIII was called "Defender of the Faith" by Pope Leo X

Mary I was known as "Bloody Mary" because she killed so many Protestants

Philip Sidney was known as the "Flower of Chivalry"

The pharaohs who built pyramids & were known as great oppressors were called "pyramid kings"

Famous Nicknames

Rameses II was known as "The Great Ancestor"

Godfrey of Bouillon was crowned "Defender of the Holy Sepulchre" after taking Jerusalem

Aeschylus was known as the "Father of Tragedy"

Appelles was known as the "Raphael of Antiquity"

Euclid was referred to as the "Father of Geometry"

Herodutus was known as the "Father of History"

Plutarch became known as "the prince of the ancient biographers"

Polykleitos' perfect sculpture was known as "the rule"

Sappho was called the "Tenth Muse" by Plato

Darius the Great has been called "the second founder of the Persian Empire"

Commodus was a "Barracks Emperor"

Fabius Maximus was known as the "Delayer"

Marcus Aurelius was the last of the "Five Good Emperors"

Atilla the Hun was known as the "Scourge of God"

Charlemagne was called "The Father of Europe"

Charles Martel was known as "Charles the Hammer" or "Martel the Hammer"

Frances Xavier was known as the "Apostle of the Indies"

Rodrigo Diaz de Vivar was better known as "the chief"

Ghenghis Khan was known as the "Universal Sovereign"

William of Orange was known as the "Prince of Orange"

Dante Alighieri's classic the Divine Comedy is considered to be the "Epic of Medievalism"

Bartolome de las Casas was known as the "Apostle of the Indians"

Accad, capital city of the Accadians, was known as the "City of Books"

Mesopotamia means "the land between two rivers"

Agamemnon was known as the "king of men"

Ajax was known as "the swift son of Oileus"

Thomas Aquinas was called the "Angel of the Schools"

The Battle of Thermopylae was known as "Hot Gates"

Historical Periods and Eras

The "Age of Tyrants":

- extended from 650 to 500 BC
- generally involved a noble tyrant who held himself out as the champion of the people but usurped the government (a tyrant was one who illegally held supreme authority in a state)

Age of Discovery

- occurred during the 15th-17th century
- during this time the Europeans engaged in intensive exploration of the world
- the Europeans established direct contact with Africa, the Americas, Asia, and Oceania
- the Age of Discovery is when the planet was mapped

The "Patriarchal Age" of Hebrew history:

- began around 2000 B.C. when Abraham left Ur of the Chaldees
- covered the lifespan of the three Hebrew patriarchs: Abraham, Isaac, and Jacob
- also included stories of Lot (Abraham's nephew) and Esau (Jacob's twin brother)

The "Middle Ages":

- is the period of history between the Dark Ages and the Renaissance
- was introduced by Italian humanists who:
    - were engaged in a revival of classical learning and culture during the 13th, 14th, or 15th century
    - believed that the 1000 years between the Dark Ages and the Renaissance (when they lived) was one of ignorance and superstition
    - wanted to separate themselves from what they saw as the age of ignorance

The "Dark Age of the Papacy":

- was a 70-year period also known as the Babylonian captivity
- began to develop when the seat of the papacy was shifted from Rome to Avignon (a city in Provence) through the efforts of Philip the Fair (a French monarch)
- resulted in all the popes being French, with all their policies being shaped and controlled by French kings

Important Dates in Chronological Order

Early Classical Ancient History:

- 776 BC: First Olympic Games, generally considered the beginning of Classical Antiquity
- 753 BC: Founding of Rome (traditional date)
- 745 BC: Tiglath-Pileser III becomes the new king of Assyria. With time he conquers neighboring countries and turns Assyria into an empire
- 722 BC: Spring and Autumn Period begins in China; Zhou Dynasty's power is diminishing; the era of the Hundred Schools of Thought
- c.750 BC: Breach of the Marib Dam in Arabia Felix (three new dams were built by the Sabaeans)
- c 728 BC: Rise of the Median Empire
- 612 BC: Attributed date of the destruction of Ninevah and subsequent fall of Assyria.
- 600 BC: Sixteen Maha Janapadas ("*Great Realms*" or "*Great Kingdoms*") emerge. A number of these Maha Janapadas are semi-democratic republics
- c. 600 BC: Pandyan kingsom in South India
- 599 BC: Mahavira, founder of Jainism is born as a prince at Kundalavana, who ruled Magadha Empire
- 563 BC: Siddhartha Gautama (Buddha), founder of Buddhism is born as a prince of the Shakya tribe, which ruled parts of Magadha, one of the Maha Janapadas.
- 551 BC: Confucius, founder of Confucianism, is born
- 550 BC: The Achaemenid Empire is founded by Cyrus the Great
- 546 BC: Cyrus the Great overthrows Croesus King of Lydia
- 544 BC: Rise of Magadha as the dominant power under Bimbisara

- 539 BC: The Fall of the Babylonian Empire, and liberation of the Jews by Cyrus the Great
- 529 BC: Death of Cyrus the Great
- 525 BC: Cambyses II of Persia conquers Egypt
- c. 512 BC: Darius I (Darius the Great) of Persia, subjugates eastern Thrace, Macedonia submits voluntarily, and annexes Libya, Persian Empire at largest extent
- 509 BC: Expulsion of the last King of Rome, founding of Roman Republic (traditional date)
- 508 BC: Democracy instituted by Cleisthenes at Athens
- c. 500 BC: Panini standardizes the grammar and morphology of Sanskrit in the text Ashtadhyayi. Panini's standardized Sanskrit is known as Classical Sanskrit
- 500 BC: Pingala develops system ranks of binary patterns
- 490 BC: Greek city-states defeat Persian invasion at Battle of Marathon
- 480-479 BC: Greek city states decisively defeat the Persians at the Battle of Salamis and the Battle of Plataea, ending once and for all the Persian threat to Greece
- 475 BC: Warring States Period begins in China as the Zhou king became a mere figurehead; China is annexed by regional warlords
- c. 469 BC: Birth of Socrates
- 465 BC: Murder of Xerxes I of Persia
- 460 BC: First Peloponnesian War between Athens and Sparta
- 449 BC: End of the Greco-Persian Wars. Macedonia, Thrace and Ionia gain independence from Achaemenid Persia
- 447 BC: Building of the Parthenon at Athens started
- 424 BC: Nanda dynasty comes to power
- 404 BC: End of Peloponnesia War between the Greek city-states
- 399 BC: February 15—The Greek philosopher Socrates is sentenced to death by Athenian authorities in Athens, condemned for impiety and the corruption of youth. He refuses to flee into exile and is sentenced to death by drinking hemlock.

Important Dates in Chronological Order

- c. 385 BC: The Greek philosopher Plato, a former disciple of Socrates, founds a philosophical school at the Akademia, from land purchased from Akademus, in Athens – later famously known as the Academy. There, Plato, and the later heads of the school, called scholarchs, taught many of the brilliant minds of the day, including the famous Greek philosopher Aristotle.
- 335 BC: The Greek philosopher Aristotle founds his philosophical school – known then as the Lyceum (named because it was located near the site of the Lyceum gymnasium in Athens) – and begins teaching there.
- 331 BC: Alexander the Great defeats Darius III of Persia in the Battle of Gaugamela
- 326 BC: Alexander the Great defeats Indian king Porus in the Battle of the Hydaspes River
- 323 BC: Death of Alexander the Great at Babylon
- 321 BC: Chandragupta Maurya overthrows the Nanda Dynasty of Magadha
- 307 BC: The Greek philosopher Epicurus founds his philosophical school, the Garden of Epicurus, outside the walls of Athens
- 305 BC: Chandragupta Maurya seizes the satrapies of Paropanisadai (Kabul), Aria (Herat), Arachosia (Qanadahar) and Gedrosia (Baluchistan) from Seleucus I Nicator, the Macedonian satrap of Babylon in return for 500 elephants
- c. 302 BC: Pandiya dynasty, Chola dynasty, and Chera dynasty rule separate areas in South India
- 294 BC: Zeno of Citium founds the philosophy of Stoicism in Athens (the philosophy derives its namesake from the fact that Zeno and his followers would regularly meet near the Stoa Poikile ("*Painted Porch*") of the Athenian agora.)
- c. 252 BC: Ashoka the Great becomes the emperor of the Mauryan Empire
- c. 252 BC: Thuc Dynasty takes over Việt Nam (then Kingdom of Âu Lạc)
- c. 249 BC: Rise of Parthia (Ashkâniân), the third native dynasty of ancient Persia

- c. 233 BC: Death of Emperor Ashoka the Great; Decline of the Mauryan Empire
- 221 BC: Construction of the Great Wall begins
- c. 220 BC: Qin Shi Huang, ruler of the Qin Dynasty, unifies China (end of Warring States Period)
- c. 220 BC: Simuka, founder of the Satavahanas dynasty, rules area in South India
- 209 BC: Kingdom of Nan Yueh is established by Tch'ao T'o (Trieu Dynasty)
- 208 BC: The Xiongnu replaces the Mongolic Donghu as the dominant tribe of the Mongolian steppe and then five years later defeats the Yuezhi in Gansu, making a cup out of the skull of their leader
- c. 206 BC: Lew Pang is proclaimed emperor (Kaou-te) and the Han Dynasty is established
- 202 BC: Scipio Africanus defeats Hannibal at Battle of Zama
- 189 BC: Artaxiad Dynasty in Armenia is founded
- c. 184 BC: Sunga Empire founded
- 149 BC–146: Third and final Punic War; destruction of Carthage by Rome
- 146 BC: Corinth in Greece was destroyed by Rome and Roman authority became supreme throughout Greece
- 140 BC: The first system of imperial examinations was officially instituted in China by the Han Dynasty emperor Han Wu Di
- c. 127 BC: Chang-Kien finds the western lands of civilisation and trading opens on routes of the Silk Road
- 111 BC: The Nam Viet Kingdom (Triệu Dynasty) is destroyed by the first Chinese domination of Viet Nam
- 95-55 BC: Tigranes the Great reigns in Armenian empire
- 53 BC: Led by General Surena, the Parthians decisively defeat a Roman invasion at the Battle of Carrhae
- 49 BC: Conflict between Julius Caesar and Pompey the Great lead to the Roman Civil War

Mid Classical Ancient History

- 44 BC: Julius Caesar murdered by Marcus Brutus and others; the end of the Roman Republic and the beginning of the Roman Empire
- 27 BC: Octavian is proclaimed *princeps* (emperor) by the Roman Senate and adopts the title Augustus (lit. "the august one")
- 6 BC: Earliest estimated date for birth of Jesus of Nazareth
- 5 BC: Birth of Jesus Christ (Ussher Chronology)
- 9: Battle of Teutoburg Forest, the Imperial Roman Army's's bloodiest defeat
- 14: Death of Emperor Augustus (Octavian), ascension of his adopted son Tiberius to the throne
- 29: Crucifixion of Jesus Christ
- 68: Year of the four emperors in Rome
- 70: Destruction of Jerusalem by the armies of Titus

World in 100 A.D.

- 117: Roman Empire at largest extent under Emperor Trajan
- 192: Kingsom of Champa in Central Viet Nam

Eastern Hemisphere in 200 A.D.

- 3rd century: The Buddhist Srivijaya Empire established in the Malay Archipelago
- 220: Three Kingdoms period begins in China after the fall of Han Dynasty
- 226: Fall of the Parthian Empire and Rise of the Sassanian Empire
- 238: Defeat of Gordian III (238–244), Philip the Arab (244–249), and Valerian (253–260), by Shapur I of Persia, and Valerian is captured

- 280: Emperor Wu established Jin Dynasty providing a temporary unity of China after the devastating Three Kingdoms period

Late Classical Ancient History

- 285: Emperor Diocletian splits the Roman Empire into Eastern and Western Empires
- 313: Edict of Milan legalized Christianity throughout the Roman Empire, and thus ended the previous state-sanctioned persecution of Christians there
- 335: Samudragupta becomes the emperor of the Gupta Empire
- 378: Battle of Adrianople, Roman army under Eastern Roman Emperor Valens is defeated by the Germanic tribes
- 395: Roman Emperor Theodosius I outlaws all pagan religions in favour of Christianity.
- 410: Alaric I sacks Rome for the first time since 390 BC
- c. 455: Skandagupta repels an Indo-Hephthalite attack on India
- 476: Romulus Augustus, last Western Roman Emperor is forced to abdicate by Odoacer, a half Hunnish and half Scirian chieftain of the Germanic Heruli; Odoacer returns the imperial regalia to Eastern Roman Emperor Zeno in Constantinople in return for the title of *dux* of Italy; traditionally, the most frequently cited date for the end of the Roman Empire (although the Eastern Roman Empire, based in Constantinople, would still continue to exist until 1453)
- 529 The Eastern Roman Emperor Justinian I ordered the prominent philosophical schools of antiquity throughout the Eastern Roman Empire (including the famous Academy in Athens, among others) to close down—allegedly, because Justinian frowned upon the pagan nature of these schools

End of Classical ancient history

The transition period from Classical Antiquity to the Early Middle Ages is known as Late Antiquity. Some key dates marking that transition are:

- 293: reforms of Roman Emperor Diocletian
- 395: the division of Roman Empire into the Western Roman Empire and Eastern Roman Empire
- 476: the fall of Western Roman Empire
- 529: closure of Platon Academy in Athens by Byzantine Emperor Justinian I

The beginning of the Middle Ages is a period in the history of Europe following the fall of the Western Roman Empire spanning roughly five centuries from AD 500 to 1000. Aspects of continuity with the earlier classical period are discussed in greater detail under the heading "Late Antiquity". Late Antiquity is a periodization used by historians to describe the transitional centuries from Classical Antiquity to the Middle Ages, in both mainland Europe and the Mediterranean world: generally from the end of the Roman Empire's Crisis of the 3rd century (c. 284) to the Islamic conquests and the re-organization of the Byzantine Empire under Heraclius.

Made in the USA
Middletown, DE
26 January 2020